GODDESS
WITH A
THOUSAND
FACES

Wild, dark
and divine
goddesses of our
ancient past

GODDESS
WITH A
THOUSAND
FACES

Jasmine Elmer

RENEGADE BOOKS

First published in Great Britain in 2024 by Renegade Books

3 5 7 9 10 8 6 4

A CIP catalogue record for this book
is available from the British Library.

Hardback ISBN 978-1-408-74824-4
C-format ISBN 978-1-408-74823-7

Typeset in Electra by M Rules
Printed and bound in Great Britain by
Clays Ltd, Elcograf S.p.A.

Papers used by Renegade Books are from well-managed forests
and other responsible sources.

MIX
Paper | Supporting
responsible forestry
FSC
www.fsc.org   FSC® C104740

Renegade Books
An imprint of Dialogue
Carmelite House
50 Victoria Embankment
London EC4Y 0DZ

The authorised representative
in the EEA is
Hachette Ireland
8 Castlecourt Centre
Dublin 15, D15 XTP3, Ireland
(email: info@hbgi.ie)

www.dialoguebooks.co.uk

Dialogue, part of Little, Brown Book Group Limited,
an Hachette UK company

For my mum, who dances in the stars with these goddesses.

Table of Contents

goddess

noun

noun: **goddess**; plural noun: **goddesses**

a female deity.

a woman who is greatly admired,
especially for her beauty.

Synonyms: a queen; a beauty; priestess;
divinity; idol.

Introduction

This whole journey is a brand spanking new one. The first of its kind, *Goddess with a Thousand Faces* will ask you to interrogate your own past through a fresh new lens. It will go further and encourage you to see yourself in these goddesses, to reclaim them; and in doing so, you may just restore yourself. It's a storytelling, historical, self-reflective extravaganza, and you should give yourself a little pat on the back for making a bloody awesome choice in picking it up. You are now part of a rebellion, a movement.

Last year I turned forty. That means I have had twenty-something years of being a woman on this planet, and it got me thinking. I looked around at this world we live in and wondered what the hell has happened? Where are all the wise women of bygone times? Where are the feminine energies of nurture, compassion and gentleness? Why is everything so toxically masculine?

With men like Andrew Tate gaining scarily high levels of

adoration among young men and women's rights torn into pieces with the reversion of Roe v. Wade in the US in mid 2022, the world seemed to be getting harder for women, not easier. Even if I looked around me, to the women I know, all I could see was rushing around, giving *everything* to *everyone* – time, resources, energy – and burning out as a result. A style of living suited to the male, a suppression and disdain for the feminine energies of the world. I felt like I was screaming into the wind, alongside every other woman I know, asking for it all to stop. Unsurprisingly then, my thinking quickly turned into anger, which then transformed into passion and purpose. What you are reading here is a result of that journey.

Like all journeys, it started out all sweetness and light. It started with me planning the mother of all parties to celebrate this milestone birthday. A deep and serious focus on the type of cocktail I wanted. Even more consideration into who I would invite. But beyond that frivolity lay something deeper. It's hard for me to pinpoint, but it felt like a yearning. A desire to find out more about my own femininity, compounded by the loss of my beautiful mum a few years before and fired up by my own role of mother to my gorgeous boy. Shit had got real, and I needed *more*. So much more. You see, something amazing happens around forty – beyond hot flushes, low libido, social invisibility, and whatever else you might have been told in the press. It's a sharp focus, a clarity and, quite frankly, an outright objection to all the BS that comes with being a woman in today's age. This is where the anger came in, the need to throw off all the roles, expectations and judgement imposed upon me since I was young, and find my own feminine identity. For me, for you, for everyone. Sod the pornstar martini, I had a book to write.

So, I decided to do what I knew best, which was to 'ancient' the shit out of it to uncover new and deeply powerful truths about our past. As an ancient world expert with over twenty years' experience in the field of classical education, I wanted to search for myself – for all of us – in untold or marginalised stories of powerful goddesses of times gone by. Of goddesses that are as ancient as human civilisation; of goddesses that are still revered all over the world today. Because if goddesses could garner such adoration in the past, perhaps by restoring their stories, I might restore parts of myself. I wanted to rebuild aspects of our femininity – regardless of biological gender, for we all possess inherent female qualities. I wanted to show people, but especially women, that there is another way. That you don't need to wait until you reach forty to uncover hidden depths and truths about yourself. I also wanted it to be a global tale, for femininity is a universal thing. Plus, I am biracial, so my mixed culture influenced my choice to think openly, widely – to think BIG. Lastly, I wanted you to have the full picture – not just a mythical retelling, but some historical context too. So, you have everything you need. No knowledge assumed, everything contained and accessible to all. I wanted a book that could fold through time and space, in a concertina effect, to find the ultimate goddess inside of us. Traverse lands, spotlight cultures that have been sidelined. Let these ladies pipe up! And guess what these goddesses have to say? All traits can be female traits. We are allowed to feel angry, be loud, embrace darkness and rebel. We are not limited to what society deems palatable: pretty, obedient and demure. And you know what? I'm owning it. All aspects of self. Sweet permission to be what you want to be when you want to be it. Writing this book has profoundly changed how I view my own ancestry, handing my power back to me. I have cried, I have laughed, I have *felt all the feelings*.

Let me expand on all this a little more. The first point is super obvious, but it needs to be said. We are a construct of our societies and have been moulded by our past. Shocker, I know. But what you might not often reflect upon is what is missed out in our history lessons. Glossed over. Relegated. And spoiler alert – it's *a lot*. Further to that, you may also not consider how various influences over time have edited our history. I am not man-bashing when I say this, but do not underestimate how patriarchy has stomped all over female stories for millennia. Put all this together and what do you get? Women's stories written out of history time and time again, lost and disregarded. I'm not saying that we know nothing of women in the past – of course we do – but how much is left to discover? What I really want for you is that you read this book and embark on your own journey of discovery. Pour over these amazing ancient goddesses and see what they are whispering to you. This is not a religious exercise; I am not suggesting that you take on any of the belief systems explored here. But take these stories into your heart and see what they illuminate inside of you.

This is why I have called this book *Goddess with a Thousand Faces*; see your own faces alongside theirs. I see you. And so do they. Rise up, emboldened by the knowledge in these pages to reclaim what is rightfully yours. Stand with them and all women. Unite in the blissful freedoms these goddesses give. For you are a goddess, and you can wear as many faces as you damn well please.

What this book isn't

Goddess with a Thousand Faces isn't an encyclopaedia, and it cannot tell you *everything* you need to know about every culture of the world! In each chapter, we will first meet our goddess through a retelling which will be based upon real source material and/or a close reflection of oral traditions. It isn't an attempt to narrow our view of a goddess by focusing on just one story, as she will likely have many myths and legends in her canon. I have selected a myth according to my personal viewpoint as to what these goddesses have to say to us; what they have to say to you. The context for each section is just that – some context for you to understand the worlds these goddesses inhabit or inhabited. I cannot tell you how many times I have encountered someone reading a mythological retelling without context, coming away confused as to what is real and what isn't. This has always seemed a real shame to me; a missing piece of a very awesome puzzle. This is why I have blazed a trail with this book, to give you both sides of the coin, so that you can make up your own mind and maybe learn something new.

The context sections cannot tell you *everything* about that culture, because, quite frankly, that is impossible unless you want a book the size of your house. And my publisher wasn't up for that so ... there will be missed topics, occasional generalisations and avoidance of academic conjecture. I do this intentionally to make this book *accessible to all*, relatable and concise, rather than an epic thesis on each culture. Similarly, let's talk footnotes, which although enlightening at times, often disrupt the flow and bog us all down in detail. It is the point of this book to encourage perspective and reflection, not to get lost in rabbit holes of academic debate or nuance (there's a place for all that, but not here). I can't bear the thought that people often regard ancient cultures as the domain of the elite, or that you have to be mad clever to study them. I say sod that, because this is our shared ancestry and it's time we took it back for ourselves. It's time for a rebrand. If you happen to know a culture in detail, or if it's your own, and find yourself frustrated at the lack of depth – please don't take that personally. It is for the greater good. However, if it does happen to be new to you, see it as a first date with that culture, a testing of the edges and overall vibe. You can always have a second or third date, or a lifelong relationship with it, learning everything there is to know, or get in the face of all those footnotes I mentioned. I've added a select bibliography to whet your appetite, for those of you who are chomping at the bit to get into it. So instead of caveating this in every chapter, I've done it here. Upfront, frank and honest. Because that's how I roll. Elephant in the room acknowledged, now we can have some real fun.

Welcome to the world of the goddess . . .

FREYJA

Viking Goddess of Sexuality, War and Magic

Freyja

Viking Goddess of Sexuality,
War and Magic

The Necklace

It all began with a walk. A simple walk. Each day I like to observe the worship of the gods at the majesty of the Godafoss waterfall in our land of fire and ice. I watch from afar – always in disguise – so they cannot know my true form. Men, women and children gather at the powerful waters as they swirl and churn, tumbling over rocks more ancient than even I. The snow dances in the breeze, glides effortlessly, until it settles on the infinite blanket of white that cover the land.

Despite its spellbinding beauty, these lands can be deadly and hard for mortals to thrive in. There is much to contend with, from the fiery mountains and deep cold winters, to isolation and inconsistent crops. Glaciers, with their bright blue glistening cores, ice sparkling in the low winter sun. I weep each time a mother who has lost yet another child comes to pray to me at this sacred place, her pain on a precipice, before it plummets down, deep and hard, like the waterfall she visits. She asks me for mercy. I grant it. I gently stroke her hair – invisible to her – but the power of my touch feels like a gentle soothing wind and her pain softens, just a little, for the briefest of moments. And so it goes, everyday like this. I see the human condition, raw and cracked open. And every day I vow to soothe their pain, in whatever way I can. You see, I have many, many talents and powers. That is why they utter my name so often in prayer. *Freyja*. And I exalt in their worship, basking in the glory they pour upon me.

Time to move on. But today it is different; I wish to take an alternative route. Little did I know that this change in direction would lead to my downfall, to my name being sullied throughout time. As I walk, I spy the entrance to a cave. A dark, black cave, created by the fire rocks that are dotted all over this land. In the middle of this blackness is a glow. It calls me. And as I get closer, I see beauty like I have ever seen before: a *Brísingamen*, a golden torc, being forged in the hot fires by four dwarves. Round in shape, glistening like the sun. Amber is being placed in adornment along its curved surface and it is then that I see that this jewellery is the essence of me, the physical form of the fire that burns inside me. When I see it, I see my power. And I need it. Now.

'How much for the necklace?' I ask the dwarf closest to me. He looks me up and down, before he shudders in recognition at my divinity. Then he gives a crooked smile. 'For the goddess Freyja there is no amount of silver or gold that could purchase this beauty.' I fix my eyes on him, and then each of them in turn, before settling on the one furthest away, the one shying away into the shadows.

'You. Speak up. I will have this necklace. What price will you accept for it?' And from the darkness, comes a sinister but clear whisper. 'You.'

I sigh. I know exactly what he is referring to. Men all across the land covet me, they see my beauty, my sexual power, and their eyes turn dark with desire. As they drink in my delicate curves, long silky flowing blonde hair and blazing blue eyes, they fall deeper and deeper into lust for me. They can think of nothing else. I find this tedious if I am honest, and pathetic that men can be manipulated so easily. All of these warriors, belittled by their swollen desire for me. Ha! It has been my currency since the dawn of time. For me, it means nothing at all. In fact, at times I enjoy it – physically, I mean. And if I am not enjoying it in that way, there is always the other way, the way of my superior power. When I use my currency, I do so with free will and always with the upper hand.

Now, I weigh up the current situation and decide that I want that necklace badly enough to pay their price. 'Very well,' I reply.

As they come towards me, one by one, I lie back and

allow them to do their bidding. The deeds are over in a flash, hardly a moment to register. Not the greatest experience, rather perfunctory, but at least now I have my necklace. I raise myself from the dusty ground, smooth off my sumptuous robes and snatch up my necklace, placing it around my delicate neck. It glows even more brightly at it touches my skin, as it mingles with the essence of my power and embodies it for eternity. I smile as my face emerges into the summer sun, burning brightly along with it.

I awoke today to find my necklace vanished, gone, missing. And along with it, my power. It must have been Loki, the shapeshifting trickster god and meddler in all divine matters. I cannot think who else would do such an awful thing. He is honestly the most irritating, treacherous being I know.

Quicker than a lightning flash, I arrive at Loki's place and blast the front door off its hinges. Rage is boiling inside me, as I set my eyes on his smug face. He is lying in front of the fire, dangling berries above his mouth with a goblet of beer beside him. He does not even bother to look up, but instead bellows: 'Leave us.' And all of his attendants scuttle away in fear of what is about to come.

Finally, he faces me. I examine his features: small inset eyes, red hair and a skinny yet tall stature. He repulses me. He interrupts my thoughts: 'What do you need, Freyja? Why are you here breaking down my doors?'

I scoff. 'Enough games, Loki; you know exactly why I am here. Give it back to me. NOW!'

At this he laughs, a hearty laugh, and the anger rises so fast within me that I start to feel giddy. I rush across the room and grab him by the scruff of his neck, lifting him high off the ground so his feet are dangling in the air.

'OK, OK. Put me down!' he exclaims. As I do so, I can feel him trembling. Fear and lust. The two responses I receive most often from men. A curious combination at times. I refocus on the moment, and realise Loki is speaking. '... and so, Odin ordered me to steal it to force you to confront him. He doesn't like sharing you with others.' Loki now looks a little sheepish. 'And he wants you to be punished for your lack of loyalty to him.' His eyes remain fixed to the ground as he splutters out this last bit.

Instead, I sigh. These men. Odin is the worst. They all want me, lust after me, but some, like him, need more. They need dominion over me. They need to own me, keep me all for themselves. But I am the one that controls my currency not them. Still, I need to play this carefully. Odin is very powerful indeed, ruler of Valhalla, the sacred halls of the dead. I need him onside.

'Take me to him, Loki. I need to speak with him at once.' Loki nods and we soar high above this land of fire and ice. Looking down, I drink in the breathtaking beauty of this place. Waterfalls, fire mountains, ice rivers and green – so much green in these summer months. This place is sacred. I cherish it the most of all of the lands we gods oversee. I believe the mortals call it Iceland. A fitting name.

We are now entering the great halls of Valhalla, where courageous warriors dwell for all eternity. Cavernous, with the accessories of war taking centre stage, areas for feasting and fighting. It's a rather intense place, even for a goddess, it makes me feel so small. Above us is a roof lined with mighty golden shields, below rows and rows of men gorging on boar's flesh in merriment.

We sink down in front of Odin, seated on his golden throne at the end of the hall. His large frame looms over us, lines of wisdom carved deep into his face, reflecting the scarred lands of this great country. His white beard the colour of snow, his solitary eye fixed down upon us. For he gave away his other eye in exchange for wisdom. His spear is propped to his side and his cloak cascades down the throne upon which his sits. I have been here many a time, flown many a soul down here to him. I notice that Odin is staring at me, rage in his eye but also something else. There is disappointment swimming there too.

I decide I must speak first: 'Odin, I have come about my necklace. What will it take for you to return it to me?' I plead with him using my words, but also my whole body.

'You have disgraced me. I took that necklace after I learned what you did to get it. I made Loki transform into a fly and sneak into your home last night, stealing it while you slept.'

I sigh, aware that I must tread carefully when dealing with the pride of a god. Even though I do not agree with him, I know I have to concede a little. It feels befitting to use my feminine wiles to persuade him; after all, that is how I keep my power.

I spend a further moment weighing up my options before I speak. Then I say, 'Odin, please forgive me. I did not mean to cause you offence. What will it take for you to return my precious Brísingamen to me? Name your price.' What a thing it is to be a woman in a man's world. Always having to negotiate, concede and pander to their fragile egos. It amuses me that they believe they hold all the power, when in reality, I am the master. I am leading Odin to wherever I want him to go. Little does he know that there is no price that I would not pay to get my precious necklace back. Still, I play the game. I shake myself back to the present, as I realise that Odin is speaking.

'I will return it to you, but the price will be high. I want you to pay in the blood of mortals. I want you to use your *seiðr*, your magic, to cast a spell on two kings to fight for eternity, until a Christian man is able to slay them and stop the curse.'

So here it is: he wants me to pay in the blood of noble men, a price he knows will sting me due to my fondness for mankind. I do not reply, but nod curtly. Loki hands me my necklace, and I rejoice in feeling its cool, smooth and heavy weight in my hands again. I run my fingers over the amber stones, and they respond by glowing brightly back at me. I close my eyes, as I snap the necklace onto my neck, like a log tossed on a dying fire, setting it ablaze once more. And so, it is in me, I burn more fiercely with it.

There is still the price to pay; Odin is getting impatient in front of me. I begin to utter the words of incantation, quietly under my breath. For it is me who gave magic to the world, the gods included and the *Völva*, the witches of our Viking world. They use my powers for all sorts of things, sometimes good and sometimes bad. Such is the way with magic, its power lies in the intent of the practitioner. As I conclude the spell, I open my eyes and see Odin beaming at me. Funny how he thinks he has won, believes that he has been successful in manipulating me. Silly men! I take my leave, floating back from whence I came. Doubt makes a passing appearance as I wonder if there is hidden price. But what choice did I really have?

One hundred and forty-three years pass. The two kings, Högni and Heðinn, are locked in an eternal battle. Each time one of them is slain, they rise again only to start the bloody fight once more. These men are in such a pitiful state, it pains me so to see their suffering. So, I decide to intervene a little – a secret I must keep for all time. I mutter under my breath and conjure him. The man who will break this curse appears: Olaf Tryggvason, the Christian. I watch on as he sweeps through the land with his armies, before sending the two kings down to Valhalla, down to Odin. It is done.

Except it was not quite done. Little did I know that the spread of this Christian faith would be in direct conflict with us, the Old Gods. Slowly, over time, fewer people came to Godafoss to seek our approval, turning instead to the Christian God. Mothers no longer wept at the banks of the waterfall, imploring me for mercy. The joy in my heart seeped away with every lost one, as we all began to fade away. Soon we became the stuff of legends – relegated to fireside entertainment. With Thor, Loki and all the other male gods taking centre stage, we female gods were made to be minor characters. And then there was the final indignity. The chroniclers began to demonise me, make me a mere whore in their eyes. Taking my sexual freedom and smearing it. They relegated and reviled me, reducing me to a side note, ripping away my true power. The people had forgotten me – there was no one left to tell of the old ways, no one left who remembered how mighty and powerful I was. I was a ghost. And I wept and wept as my agency was stolen from me, my sexuality and power rebranded as a sin. My gift of magic, which I had given to the people, to the Völva – the seeresses – was hunted down and extinguished. These women were tortured, vilified, alongside me.

A man called Þorgeir dealt the final blow. He came one day to Godafoss, clutching the idols of us Old Gods in his hands. The people gathered and watched on as he publicly denounced the old pagan ways and threw the idols in the great waterfall, proclaiming the country of Iceland a Christian one. Since that day I have not left the banks of this waterfall. I sit and wait, tears falling with the churning waters, for someone to utter my name, desperate for someone to recall my glory. I clasp the necklace in my hand, dull now with the loss of my power. I reminisce on the times it used to glow. If you sit here, you may hear me calling to you on the cool summer breeze. As you gaze into the icy blue waters, you may recall my eyes. If you stay here long enough, I may be reborn. I will wait, hoping you will come and remember me.

Freyja's World

This retelling was a tough one. It is based on a late-fourteenth-century text called *Sörla þáttr*. An Icelandic saga co-authored by Christian writers, it is a captivating narrative that indeed offers a glimpse into the rich cultural heritage of Iceland. However, it is not without its problems. One notable issue is the potential anachronisms that might arise from the incorporation of Christian themes and values into a tale set in a pre-Christian Norse context. The blending of Christian elements into a saga that might have originally revolved around pagan beliefs can lead to a discordant narrative and raise questions about the authenticity of the story's cultural representation. Additionally, the influence of Christian authors might introduce bias or selective reinterpretation of certain events or characters to align them with Christian morality. This could compromise the saga's original integrity and message, altering the story's core essence for religious or didactic purposes. Moreover, the infusion of Christian themes into a narrative rooted in Norse mythology could risk undermining the cultural significance and uniqueness of the Icelandic sagas as a reflection of the Norse worldview. Critics might argue that such amalgamation contributes to the homogenisation of cultural narratives. Lastly, the involvement of Christian authors could lead to the exclusion or downplaying of aspects that did not align with Christian beliefs. This selective retelling could overlook valuable cultural insights or historical elements that were present in the original version, resulting in a biased representation of the past.

So, you can see how hard it is to find our goddess in all of this. It is why I chose to add the ending to allow us to reflect on how she has been forgotten, sidelined and maligned by such authors. This is not necessarily unique to Freyja – almost all of our goddesses could lay claim to this to some extent – but may her story allow you to spend a moment in contemplation of voices lost. This is symbolic of how many other female narratives have been misappropriated, ignored and erased throughout history. It makes me sad and angry. And it's why I wanted to write this book.

Step with me into the world of the Vikings, a society bustling with adventure, exploration, and a unique social structure. Imagine lands of vast and towering landscapes, of fire and ice, where mighty warriors set sail on magnificent longships, sails billowing in the wind. That's what we picture, isn't it? A culture ruled by fearsome warriors who would absolutely nail Ultimate Fighter Championships today. Straight off the bat, I am not trying to argue that this wasn't the case. It is accurate to say that Viking culture was intensely male oriented, martially driven (although to what degree we must remain open minded) and largely illiterate. The last word there is not a slur, it is relative truth according to the evidence we have. Vikings did not record their thoughts, so we must rely heavily on later Scandinavian sources – which are often Christian, making the authentic Viking voice a tad elusive. What we do know is pieced together by later histroical works, archaeology and, possibly most problematically, people from outside the culture (like the Romans). What I am stating is that much of Viking culture has been relegated to clichés and stereotypes – yes, just like the one I started with – and it's important that we wade through that to examine a nuanced and complex culture, one beyond the clashing of swords and plaiting of hair.

However, what we do know is this: the Vikings were a diverse group of people originally hailing from Scandinavia, consisting of Norway, Sweden and Denmark, and dating between eighth and eleventh centuries CE. They populated many other areas, including Iceland, parts of France and Britain. Many argue they traded much further afield than this, possibly as far as Arabia and into areas of modern Russia, according to the latest work on the evidence of coinage. They also crossed the Atlantic and founded settlements on Greenland and into North America – the site of L'Anse aux Meadows is a Viking settlement in Newfoundland that dates to at least 1021 CE. So, all of this paints an intricate picture, a growing network of colonies, all of which develop their own distinctly regional variant of 'Vikingness' (yes, I made that word up).

The focus of Viking society was multifaceted. Firstly, exploration and expansion were key objectives for the Vikings. They sought to discover new lands, establish trade routes and secure resources through expeditions and overseas settlements. This drive for expansion was fuelled by a desire for wealth, power and prestige. Additionally, the Vikings aimed to uphold their social order and maintain a strong sense of honour and reputation. This involved demonstrating bravery in battle, adhering to societal customs and laws, and fulfilling their obligations to their families and communities. Another important aim of Viking society was the pursuit of wisdom and knowledge. They placed great emphasis on storytelling, poetry and oral tradition, valuing wisdom and sagacity as important virtues. Furthermore, the Vikings sought to ensure the well-being and prosperity of their kin. They engaged in agriculture, animal husbandry and trade to secure a comfortable standard of living.

Religion played a significant role in Viking society, with their beliefs revolving around a pantheon of gods and goddesses. They worshipped deities such as Odin, Thor and our goddess Freyja, attributing natural phenomena, battles and prosperity to their divine influence. Much of the literary evidence we have today explores this rich mythology, such as the *Poetic Edda* and *Prose Edda*, collections of myths in either verse or prose form. Religious ritual would have been at the centre of daily Viking life, and women held key roles as part of this worship as spiritual and religious figures. These were often the Völva that we mentioned in the story – a group of people, often women, that became respected seeresses in Viking communities. We will get into them a little later on. The Vikings held grand religious gatherings called Things, where matters of law, governance and disputes were resolved. Yes, it was really called a *þing* (Thing), which could also mean an inanimate object in Proto-Germanic languages, but here it is used to denote a meeting or concern. Picture these Things as vibrant assemblies, where individuals came together to shape the destiny of their society. In fact, most aspects of daily Viking life would be discussed at these meetings, and you can imagine them as busy, loud events, with men and women from the community debating passionately. Daily life would also consist of agricultural duties, probably taken on by the men; women tended to work inside, devoted to domestic chores, cooking, childcare and weaving. In this sense, gender roles were rather rigidly defined.

In Viking society, everyone had a place, and that place was determined by their social class. There were three main classes: *Thralls, Karls* and *Jarls*. Envisage this as a pyramid, with Thralls at the bottom, Karls in the middle and Jarls at the top. This social hierarchy reflected the roles and responsibilities individuals held within the community. The Thralls were essentially enslaved people, performing essential tasks for the community. They worked on farms, in households, and were involved in construction projects. They laboured hard, but their status was despised, and they were looked down upon by society. Some Thralls were captured during Viking raids on neighbouring European societies, and were therefore prisoners of war, while others were born into servitude. Moving up the pyramid, we encounter the Karls, who were the free peasants. These hardworking individuals owned farms, land and cattle. Picture them tilling the soil, milking cows and constructing homes and wagons. They led lives of toil and dedication, ensuring the sustenance and well-being of their families and communities. While they enjoyed freedom, Karls often relied on Thralls to assist with their workload. At the pinnacle of the social structure were the Jarls, the aristocracy of Viking society. Jarls were wealthy landowners who possessed vast estates, grand longhouses and noble titles. Imagine them riding on horseback, their presence commanding respect and admiration. They were responsible for the administration of their territories, engaging in politics, hunting and sports. Jarls were held in high regard, and their influence reached far and wide. In addition to these three classes, Viking society had a range of intermediate positions, allowing for some social mobility. Individuals could transition between the Karls and Jarls, acquiring different titles and positions along the way. It was a society where one's status could evolve through various roles and achievements. Within this social framework, the Vikings also formed communities known as *félag*. These were tight-knit groups centred around shared interests, such as trade, seafaring or military obligations. It was within these spheres that camaraderie, trust and cooperation thrived.

We have already touched upon the lives of women, but let's delve a little deeper. In Viking society, women faced similar challenges as women in medieval Europe. They were often subordinate to their husbands and fathers, lacking significant political power. However, there were instances where Viking women enjoyed more freedom and independence compared to women in other regions. Most free Viking women were primarily housewives, and their social status was closely tied to their husbands. Marriage provided them with a level of economic security and social standing, and they were recognised as the 'lady of the house'. Norse laws acknowledged their authority over the household, including managing resources, conducting business and raising children, although some responsibilities were shared with their husbands. Once an unmarried woman reached the age of twenty, she attained legal majority and had the right to choose her place of residence. She was regarded as an individual with her own rights before the law, although marriage arrangements were typically made by the family. Marriages involved a bride-price paid by the groom to the bride's family, and the bride would bring assets into the marriage as a dowry. Divorce and remarriage were possible for married women.

Concubinage also existed in Viking society, allowing a woman to live with a man and have children without being married. These women, called *friðla*, were usually from lower classes, including enslaved people, and often had relationships with wealthy and powerful men who already had wives. The wife held authority over the concubines if they lived in her household. While a concubine and her family could advance socially through the relationship, her position was less secure than that of a wife. Children born both inside and outside of marriage had inheritance rights, and there was no distinction between legitimate and illegitimate children, although those born within wedlock had greater claims to inheritance. Upon the death of her husband, a woman had the right to inherit part of his property. Widows enjoyed the same independent status as unmarried women. Certain female relatives, such as the paternal aunt, niece and granddaughter, also had inheritance rights. In the absence of a husband, sons or male relatives, a woman could inherit property and assume the position of the head of the family upon the death of her father or brother. This woman, known as *Baugrygr*, exercised all the rights of a family clan's leader until her marriage, at which point her rights transferred to her husband. There is some conjecture about another group of women that have their roots in Norse mythology and folklore – that of the shield maiden. The shield maiden had warrior status and fought in battles. There is some evidence for this being historically accurate – some argue that weapons have been found next to females in burials. There are also historical texts to suggest that shield maidens existed; however, between myth, legend and history, it is hard to provide a conclusive answer.

In the domestic sphere, women at the lower end of the social structure engaged in textile and jewellery making.

These women spent their days weaving cloths for clothing, rugs and blankets, so essentially they were responsible for keeping people warm and alive in such harsh climates. In such a way, it might be argued that women formed the basis for a huge portion of the North Atlantic trade and economy. Similarly, jewellery makers were highly skilled and respected, creating ornate and beautiful pieces admired far beyond Viking lands. But perhaps the most interesting aspect of their lives would have been their association with religion and the freedom that religion offered them.

The most tantalising of religious context was that of magical. In Viking belief, sorcery (both good and bad) was in the firm power of the feminine. It was not customary for men to be involved in any area of life that was considered feminine, as it would affect the masculinity of the man in question. That is not to say men could not or did not partake in magical ritual, however in the wider context of Viking thought, it would have been frowned upon. In the realm of magic, women played a prominent and respected role as seeresses, as we have already discovered. These seeresses held a special connection to the supernatural, believed to possess the ability to communicate with the gods and tap into hidden knowledge. They were like the wise women of their time, offering guidance, divination and healing to their communities. Seeresses engaged in divination, a practice that allowed them to peer into the future and unravel mysteries. They used various techniques such as rune reading, interpreting dreams and scrying (looking into objects or surfaces for divine messages) to unlock the secrets of the unknown. Imagine consulting a seeress for a glimpse into your future or seeking their insight on important life decisions. Their ability to offer guidance and prophecies added an element of enchantment to Viking society.

The power of seeresses extended beyond mere divination. They possessed remarkable healing abilities that blended herbal knowledge with magical practices. Using a combination of herbs, charms and incantations, they worked to restore health and alleviate suffering. These incantations may have involved calling upon a god or goddess, especially our goddess Freyja, to assist with the spell or healing in question. Runes, a Germanic system of language, were used in a magical context to provide divine insight. A bit like Tarot today, the seeress would throw the symbols up into the air and decipher their meaning as they landed. There might also have been chanting, music and singing. Think of these individuals not necessarily as witches, but as skilled healers, drawing upon the forces of nature and the unseen world to bring comfort and well-being to those in need. The influence of seeresses was not limited to individual matters; they also played a role in the social and political fabric of Viking society. Kings and chieftains sought their counsel on matters of governance, wars and alliances. A seeress could advise a ruler on a pivotal decision, their words carrying the weight of divine wisdom. Their presence in the political sphere highlights the esteem and trust placed in their magical abilities.

Magic and the role of seeresses challenged traditional gender roles, giving women a unique place of power and influence. In a time when societal expectations for women were often limited, the Vikings celebrated and respected the feminine connection to the mystical. This recognition empowered women and set Viking society apart from other cultures of the era. Beyond its impact on individuals and society, magic held a profound spiritual significance. It connected the Vikings to a world of gods, giants and mythical beings. Magic was seen as a means to communicate with these realms, reinforcing the belief in a vibrant and interconnected cosmos. It added a sense of wonder to their worldview, a reminder of the hidden forces that shaped their lives.

Freyja held immense importance in Viking society, occupying a central position in their pantheon of gods and goddesses. Her significance stemmed from her association with love, beauty, fertility and the magical practice of seiðr. Freyja's multifaceted nature and her domain over fundamental aspects of human existence made her a revered and cherished figure among the Vikings. One of Freyja's key roles was that of a love and fertility deity. She embodied desire, passion and sensuality, and her presence was believed to bless unions and foster fruitful relationships. Freyja's association with love and sexuality made her a vital figure in matters of the heart. Couples would often seek her favour in matters of love, courtship and marriage, believing that her guidance would lead to fulfilling and harmonious relationships. Fertility was another essential aspect of

Freyja's domain. She was seen as the patroness of fertility, in terms of both human procreation and the abundance of nature. Her blessings were sought after by those desiring children or seeking agricultural prosperity. My retelling above has tried to reinstate this goddess in alignment with the evidence we have for her widespread worship and close ties to sexuality. Far from being vilified for her sexual prowess, she was championed and adored for it.

Her importance for female fertility becomes more understandable when we consider the analysis of Viking-era burials and skeletal remains. Studies indicate that the average lifespan for women during this period ranged from approximately thirty-five to forty-five years. It is crucial to note that these numbers are estimates and can vary based on factors such as geographic location, social status and overall health. Skeletal remains provide valuable insights into the physical toll of Viking women's lives, showcasing signs of wear and tear on bones (skeletal damage), evidence of childbirth complications and indications of manual labour. These findings suggest that Viking women led physically demanding lives, engaged in various activities such as farming, weaving and household chores, which likely contributed to their lower life expectancy compared to their male counterparts. This underscores Freyja's role in ensuring the continuation of life and the prosperity of the community. If we consider that these women may also have consulted the Völva, we can see the presence of our goddess again, guiding these women in their times of need through the practice of seiðr.

Freyja's importance in Viking society was further emphasised by her widespread worship and the rituals in honour
of her. Temples and shrines were dedicated to her, and she
was venerated through rituals, offerings and festivals. Old
Norse sources don't explicitly mention a cult of Freyja, but
there are many place names across Sweden and Norway
that relate to her name, such as *Frovi* (Freyja's shrine)
and *Froihov* (Freyja's temple). This hints at the presence
of a more official cultic worship of her. Archaeological
discoveries have shed light on the worship and cult of
Freyja, providing valuable clues about the veneration of
her and her significance within Norse mythology. The
discovery of amulets and pendants associated with Freyja
further highlights her importance. These amulets, often
in the shape of cats or falcons (some of her symbols), were
believed to represent Freyja and were worn by individuals
for protection and devotion. The presence of such amulets
in burials and hoards suggests that Freyja was revered not
only as a powerful deity but also as a guardian and guide
for the living and the deceased. The prominence of amulets and pendants indicates that Freya's worship extended
beyond the realm of mythology and played a tangible role
in the daily lives of the Vikings, demonstrating the deep
devotion and reliance on Freyja's protection. This is why
I felt the need to reinstate her as goddess of the people in
my retelling.

So, to you. What can her story gift to you? Freyja's tale
is a warning in so many ways. Firstly, she has something to

tell us about our ownership of our sexuality. Freyja was a goddess who had sexual agency; she made her own choices and honoured herself through such choices. She teaches us to reflect on how much of our own sexual behaviour has been defined by patriarchal conditions laid down upon us. How the branding of a young woman who chooses sexual freedom has been directed towards judgement and disgust for centuries. What Freyja tells us is to create our own lives and reclaim the potency of our sexuality, without the veil of societal criticism. Female sexual power should be embraced, not reviled and supressed. In the modern world, women are constantly 'slut shamed'. With the rise of obsession with 'body count'— a popular term for the number of sexual partners a person has had – it doesn't seem that we will be abandoning our judgement of women and their sexual endeavours any time soon. In addition to this, women are faced with the fears that surround 'revenge porn', the practice of scorned lovers sharing intimate photos or videos in public and importantly, without consent. In the UK, only 825 cases of revenge porn were charged by the Crown Prosecution Service between April 2020 and June 2022. A horrifically low number given how entrenched this issue seems to be, especially among young teenage girls. It appears that the boundaries of free sexual expression for women are closing in, not expanding. We could all learn a lot from Freyja in this respect.

Freyja offers us even more than this. She asks us to pay heed to who we allow to tell our stories. When we allow others to speak for us, we lose our agency and power. How can we as women reclaim our own stories, not just about our sexual selves, but beyond? Consider for a moment: how authentically do you use your own voice? Do you speak your truth no matter what? How often have you felt silenced, unable to stand up for yourself? Reflect upon what restricts you, and question whether that is the right path. Freyja wants us to be more authentic – to be our truest selves.

ARTEMIS

Greek Goddess of the Wild, Hunting, Childbirth and Virginity

Artemis

Greek Goddess of the Wild,
Hunting, Childbirth and Virginity

The Punishment

I'm running. Speckled sunlight dances across my body as it sparkles through the gaps in the trees. My feet pound the ground, dust flicking up in my wake. Deeper and deeper into the glade, through the thick of trees said to be as old as time. Ahead of me I see a clearing and as I reach it, I collapse into the long, silky grass. My heart is thudding in my ears as I take in long deep breaths of the cold mountain air, a scent of pine and dampness. My dress is a mess, now covered in stains from my forest running, from my rough and tumble. My golden band is off-centre on my head – I adjust it. I glide my fingers along my bow, my trusty companion that accompanies me on every jaunt, on every hunt. I unhook its cover, a soft blood-red case, which I fold up and place behind my head. I stare directly above, eyes following the long lines of tree trunks all the way up as they explode into fluffy green clouds against the backdrop of a bright blue sky. Joy fills my being. I am home.

I awaken. The sun is glistening through the trees, shards of light dancing around me. Although day has only just broken, I can feel the intense heat of the sun warming my skin already. Beads of sweat form on my collar bone and meander along the curves of my breasts. It is sticky hot, and I am suddenly grateful to be embraced by the cooler air of the mountain. It must be stifling down in the cities right now, but Mount Cithaeron is known for its lush pine forests and temperate climate. That is why I like to hunt here. It is also teeming with life. Deer, rabbits and wolves roam freely, all fair game for me – their goddess. This wilderness is my domain; the very essence of me permeates all living things that reside here. It has always been hard to see where I end and nature begins.

The Oreads – mountain nymphs – approach me, in their ethereal glow; young women of such majestic beauty that they are often under the oppressive gaze of men. Each of them born from the nature that surrounds us – clouds, trees, springs, caverns, meadows and beaches. Each of them is the physical manifestation of these powerful energies, bound to protect. The Oreads assemble around me, as we stand in a circle in the same clearing that I raced through yesterday. The heat is prickling the back of my neck and I begin to slowly take off my clothes. The nymphs do the same.

Without exchanging words, we all know what it is we wish to do: dive into the cool waters of the pool which lies before us. Its deep blue hues call us, enticing us with its refreshment. The water is so clear I can see all the way to the bottom. It is lined with rocks, of varying sizes, too deep for me to feel with my feet. The enchantment of the pool beckons, as I throw down the last of my robes and stand naked beside it, savouring the breeze on my skin before I plunge into the cool depths. Submerged, I see the nymphs jump in too, hearing squeals of delight as the cool water soothes their hot skin. Like when a storm rolls in and quenches parched lands, we are sated. And all the while, in the purity of this moment, we had no idea that we are being watched.

A scream. I hear it even from beneath the water. I swim hard to reach the surface, and as my head emerges, so does another. Two of the nymphs stand by the side of the pool, holding up their robes to cover their bare bodies, mouths agape, eyes bulging and fixed in one direction: beyond the trees, some short distance from the pool. It is the sound of barking hounds that gives him away first, before I catch sight of him and bore my eyes into his.

He stands there, as still as a statue, bow and quiver thrown down by his side, hunting knife affixed to his leather belt. A hint of a strong chest beneath his tunic. Dark brown hair running down his back, eyes like glistening bronze shields, skin the colour of golden dawn. He is holding his breath. He watches me. And I watch back as his eyes begin to transform: at first full of desire, now flooding with fear. He realises what he has done, and no doubt what is to come next. It is then that I spring out of the water, still naked, and quickly throw my robes back on. My eyes never leave his. He knows his time is up, so he breaks eye contact and begins to run. But you cannot outrun a goddess; he should know this.

It takes only a moment, one moment to break a man's life. For there is nothing that I guard more fiercely than my reputation, my chastity and my purity. I will not allow this man's lust to pollute my body. I look up and notice the nymphs have scattered, fled in shame and embarrassment, but perhaps also fear as to what will come next.

The words are spoken as he returns to me – Actaeon – once a celebrated and loved hunter, a man I truly admired for his prowess. My magic rips him of his manly appearance, and he stands before me as a stag. Now, a wild animal, head bowed low, he plods towards me. Eyes no longer full of fear or desire, but sadness and remorse. He stands before me for a moment, goddess and animal together as one, as we both understand what is to come next.

'Run,' I tell him, as he turns away from me and pounds the ground as hard and fast as I have ever seen, the realisation that he is no longer predator but now prey. His once beloved hounds catch the scent of him in their nostrils, as he has spent many years training them to do. Unaware that this stag is their adored master, they make chase and catch up with him in no time at all. I watch, as they pounce upon him, horror awash in his eyes. First they bite and scratch the layers of his fur, to reveal bright red bloody sinews and muscles, then they tear their way through his body, clawing deeper and deeper, ripping his flesh, until he is fully torn open and parts of him lay strewn across the forest floor. The lush green is saturated with bright red blood. Eyes now dull, life has left him.

I pick up my bow and quiver, reset my headdress, and begin to stroll through the pine forest. The once cool and calm mountain air is now singed with the smell of death. I exalt. I delight in the destruction of this predator. For he had no right to look upon me, a goddess, a pure being. The punishment fits the crime. Treat me like prey, I will show you what it feels like to be stalked by a predator. I smile. I feel my power pulsating through my veins. For my virginity is for me to own and no one else. I am the driver of my own destiny. The lusts of men are no match for a goddess. Cross me, and I will tear you apart.

Artemis's World

The retelling above is based on numerous Ancient Greek sources that tell this very famous story of Artemis. Like most Greek myths, it comes in many different versions, adapted and moulded by the storytellers that have told it. You see, it is commonplace for myths to change over time, to reflect new ideas, explore new notions, or to entertain in a new and interesting way. As such, there is no one 'correct' version of a myth. Think of it as a tree, its trunk forming the main basis of the story, like the characters and general plot, but an individual storyteller can choose which branch to travel, and how to embellish this branch with leaves. These leaves are the specifics of the story, like description and exploring the motivations of a character. In such a way, I have continued this tradition; I have followed the main trunk, but I have imagined Artemis's emotional response to Acteon. The brutal punishment here, though, is all Greek, and attested in many ancient sources, such as Aeschylus, Pseudo-Apollodorus and Ovid.

Full immediate disclosure – as we have so much evidence from Ancient Greek culture, it will be hard to do it justice in a chapter of this size. However, I will endeavour to give you a decent outline before we delve into the worship of our fabulous goddess. While there were a number of pre-historic people living across Europe originally, a distinctly 'Greek' culture began to flourish on the island of Crete around 3000 BCE with the Minoan civilisation. This was followed by the domination of Mycenaean culture, which dates from around 1600–1100 BCE. With an intervening so-called 'Dark Age', Greek culture began to re-emerge. By around 700 BCE, this civilisation had developed and spread across the Greek Islands and into the Greek mainland. This was the latterly named 'Archaic period', which was characterised by the development of city-states and the rise of Greek culture and art. The Greeks developed to be a people who valued independence, democracy and excellence in all areas of life, including politics, philosophy and athletics. It is important to note that Ancient Greece was not a homogenous society, but rather a collection of diverse city-states with their own unique customs and traditions, changing over time. These city-states often competed with one another, both culturally and militarily, but they also shared a common language, religion and cultural heritage. This is probably the Greece you conjure up in your mind of temples, sculptures, philosophers and athletes.

We can't talk Ancient Greece without jumping straight to one of the most influential of these city-states: Athens. It emerged as a powerful city-state by around the 400s BCE and became a centre of intellectual and artistic development, making lasting contributions to Western civilisation. It was governed by a democratic system that was developed by various Greek statesmen, such as Solon and Pericles, between roughly 594 and 355 BCE. Citizens of Athens had the right to participate in the government, which was composed of an assembly of all male citizens over the age of eighteen. Not surprisingly, women or enslaved people were not eligible to vote. More on that later. The assembly met several times a month to discuss and vote on important issues, such as war and peace, taxation and legislation. One of the most famous leaders of Athens was Pericles, who governed the city-state during the Golden Age of Athens between around 461 and 429 BCE. The city was also a military power, with a powerful navy that allowed it to control much of the Aegean Sea. The Athenian army was composed of citizen-soldiers who were trained in the use of weapons and tactics. Athens was involved in several major conflicts during its history, including the Persian Wars, the Peloponnesian War and the Macedonian Wars. In addition to its political and military achievements, Athens was known for its cultural contributions. Athenian literature, philosophy and art continue to be studied and admired to this day. Athens was also a centre of scientific and mathematical discovery. The Athenian method of education, which emphasised the study of rhetoric, music and athletics in a private setting, was also influential in shaping Western education. Athens was a city-state that made significant contributions to Western civilisation in the areas of politics, culture and military power. Its democratic government, cultural achievements and military continue to be studied and admired to this day, and its legacy has endured for thousands of years.

The 'nemesis' of Athens was the city of Sparta – you might know those muscly guys from the movie 300. Sparta was known for its military might and strict social system. Unlike Athens, which had a democratic government, Sparta was ruled by a small group of aristocrats known as the *Spartiates*. The Spartiates were an elite class of citizens who were trained from a young age in the art of warfare. Boys were taken from their families at the age of seven and placed in military barracks where they received rigorous physical training and were taught to be obedient to their superiors. This training was designed to create a disciplined and fearless army that could defeat any enemy.

I cannot underline enough how brutal the training was for the young boy. Being taken away from home and the safety of family, thrown out into the wilderness to encourage a so-called 'tough' exterior, facing starvation and thirst – as a mother to a seven-year-old boy, I cannot imagine how traumatic this experience would be for such a young mind. For the Spartans, it was a necessary process for young boys to go through, in order to create a fighting machine that could uphold the security of the Spartan state.

Spartan society was highly stratified, with the Spartiates at the top, followed by the *Perioikoi*, who were free but had limited rights, and the *Helots*, who were enslaved people. The Helots were an important part of Spartan society as they provided labour for the Spartiates and allowed them to focus on their military training. Despite its focus on military strength, Sparta was not a major cultural centre like Athens – it did not focus on producing great works of art or literature. However, Spartan society did have its own unique culture, with a strong emphasis on discipline, obedience and physical fitness. Sparta was involved in several major conflicts during its history, including the Persian Wars and the Peloponnesian War. Its military prowess allowed it to defeat Athens and become the dominant power in Greece during the Peloponnesian War. However, Sparta's victory was short-lived, and it eventually fell into decline as other city-states rose to power.

But what of wider Greek society? How were these people living? The social structure of Greece by the 400s BCE was divided into several classes, with a hierarchy of power and influence that was largely based on birth and wealth. It must be clearly stated here that Greece at this time was a patriarchy, so much of what I am going to ask you to imagine will more likely relate to the lives of men rather than women.

At the top of the social structure were the aristocrats. If you were lucky enough to be an aristocrat, or *aristoi* in Ancient Greek, you would be among the wealthiest and most powerful members of society. You would own large estates, have multiple enslaved people and hold political and military positions of influence. The aristocracy was a hereditary class, meaning that their power and status were passed down through their family lineage. Below the aristocracy were the common people, or the *demos*. This class was made up of free citizens who were not part of the aristocracy. If you were common, you'd be paying taxes, serving in the military and participating in the government, although not in the leading roles. You would have fewer rights and privileges than the aristocracy, but you were still able to participate in the democratic process and hold public office. But let's be frank, lots of this power was illusionary. Early democracy is a great idea *in principle* but given that universal rights to vote weren't granted until the twentieth century in most Western countries, it was more façade than reality. The lowest class in Ancient Greek society was that of the enslaved people, or *Douloi*. If you were unfortunate enough to be in this class, you were forced to work long, punishing hours and had no legal rights. You would be seen legally as a commodity, traded, sold and owned as if you were an object. Enslaved people were typically captured in war or were born into slavery, and were often used as labourers in agriculture, mining and household tasks. Slavery in Ancient Greece was based on the concept of 'natural slavery'. The idea was that some people were naturally inferior and were meant to serve others. A horrifying thought … Despite their lack of legal rights, some enslaved people in Ancient Greece were able to gain their freedom. This was usually done by purchasing their freedom from their owner, although some enslaved people were freed as a reward for their services or for a particularly brave act. Once freed, former enslaved people were known as 'freedmen' and were able to participate in some aspects of society. This is all part of the dark past upon which empires are often built. Slavery was an essential component to Greek society so it is all too easy to speak of enslaved people flippantly, but we must take a moment to reflect that these were the lives of normal men, women and children, which is deeply saddening. Another notable group in Ancient Greek society was the *Metics*, or resident aliens. Not the outer space kind – these were people who lived in Greek cities but were not citizens. They were allowed to own property, engage in trade and participate in some aspects of civic life. They were an important part of Athenian society, providing a valuable source of labour and commerce. They were also subject to Athenian laws and were required to pay taxes.

Now we haven't yet mentioned a group that made up half of the population – women! They sat across all of these social classes and as such, their life experiences were on a spectrum. Women were not considered equal to men and had limited rights and freedoms. The role of women varied depending on factors such as social class, location and time period. As a woman in Ancient Greece, you were generally considered inferior to your male counterparts, and you'd be expected to fulfil the traditional roles of wife, mother and homemaker. However, the exact nature of your role and the extent of your freedom differed depending on your circumstances. In Athens, for example, women had limited rights and freedoms. You were not considered a citizen and had no political power. Your primary role was to manage the household and bear children. Having children was extremely dangerous for women, with a high chance of dying from childbirth, and infant mortality was even higher. Average life expectancy was low (in modern terms), as you'd likely not see you thirty-fifth birthday. You were expected to be chaste and modest, and your behaviour would be strictly regulated by social norms and moral codes. You'd live in your own separate quarters and need male permission and accompaniment to leave the home. Being confined to the home, you were not allowed to participate in public life, except in certain circumstances, such as a religious context. In some cases, you could become a priestess, taking on an important role within a temple and overseeing the worship of whichever goddess you served. You may, as a part of this role, take a leading role in various ceremonies and rituals, or even become an oracle, a special kind of priestess who could speak directly to the gods. As such, you could wield great power, advising important male leaders on their next move, although these roles would have been reserved for the privileged few. As ordinary women, you might enjoy some freedoms if you were involved in a religious cult. That word did not carry the same weight as it does today, so there's no need to imagine scandalous religious groups. A cult was just the specific – and often secret – ritualistic worship of a deity. In the Ancient Greek context, they are actually referred to as 'mysteries'. Many of the goddesses had cults associated with them, and because they were often a closed membership, we don't always know what people got up to in them. You needed to be initiated into the cult in order to gain its full access and wisdom. The role of women in the cult of Artemis (and other deities) is really important, as it may have been one of the few spaces where women could be free of the male gaze.

However, it's inaccurate to say that being a woman was this restricted all over Greece. For example, in Sparta, women had a slightly different role. Because Spartan society placed a strong emphasis on military training, women were encouraged to maintain physical fitness. This was because physically fit mothers were believed to produce strong and healthy children. As a Spartan woman, you would be in peak physical health, allowed to wear short skirts – I know, shocking – and participate in athletic events. As the men focused on fighting and training, they tended to live in military barracks, so you would likely be alone in the house unless your man came along for a nightly visit, shall we say. Due to men's absence in domestic contexts in Sparta, women were allowed to own property and engage in some commercial activities. In many ways, women in Sparta appeared to have more autonomy and power than their sisters throughout Greece.

Despite their limited roles, some women in Ancient Greece were able to gain recognition for their achievements. The poet Sappho, for example, was highly respected in her time and is still celebrated for her contribution to literature. Aspasia, a member of the famous Greek statesman Pericles's household, was admired for her political cunning and intelligence. Similarly, Olympias, who was mother to Alexander the Great, reportedly influenced her son greatly. She even killed off Alexander's rival to the throne to ensure her son's position. Women in Athens were also known for their skills in weaving and pottery, which were highly valued in society. It's worth noting that the role of women in Ancient Greece was not static and changed over time. For example, during the Hellenistic period (323–31 BCE), women were able to participate more in public life and had greater opportunities for education and social mobility. However, these changes were not universal, and the exact nature of women's roles continued to vary depending on their location and social status. But I will not sugar coat it; it wasn't a great time to be a woman, which is why religious cults, like that of Artemis, were so important for women to be able to participate in and express themselves.

In addition to its political and social institutions, Ancient Greece was also renowned for its architecture, sculpture and other forms of art. One of the most famous examples of Greek architecture is the Parthenon, a temple dedicated to the goddess Athena that was built in Athens between 447–432 BCE. The Parthenon is known for its sophisticated design and exquisite marble sculptures, which were created by the renowned Greek sculptor Phidias. Greek art was also known for its depiction of the human form, which was idealised and stylised to emphasise physical perfection and beauty. These advancements in art and architecture are what we imagine when we think of Ancient Greece. If you ever have the chance, I highly recommend a trip to any of the sites in Greece to really lap up the atmosphere of these places. Delphi is a firm favourite of mine, with some stunning remains that really give you sense of the magic of the place.

Greece's aesthetic ideal was reflected in the love of athletics, which were an integral part of Greek life. The ancient Olympic Games, which were held every four years in Olympia, were the most famous athletic competition in the ancient world. They included events such as running, wrestling and chariot racing, and they were open only to male athletes. They even performed naked to show off their, er, amazing bodies to the patron of the games, mighty Zeus. It is very easy to see how the Greek obsession with the perfection and beauty of the male form inspired so many of the sculptures you might envisage when we speak of this culture. Not to mention, for me, as a former teacher, the sniggers of embarrassment from teenage boys and girls seeing them for the first time.

Greek culture was also renowned for its literature and philosophy. Literature included epic poetry, such as the works of Homer, and plays, such as those of Aeschylus, Sophocles and Euripides. They provide us with a wonderful insight into various elements of Greek life. If you are keen, many of them are still performed today – all you need to do is choose the genre – comedy or tragedy. If that isn't your bag, then perhaps you might prefer musing over those famous Greek philosophical teachings. Philosophy was marked by a focus on reason, logic and the search for knowledge. Prior to this, there was great emphasis on the supernatural to explain the glorious world that we inhabit. The philosophers of Ancient Greece, including Socrates, Plato and Aristotle, laid the groundwork for many of the ideas that would shape Western thought for centuries to come.

Let us turn our attention now to the beliefs of these people. Ancient Greek religion was a polytheistic belief system. The Greeks believed in a pantheon of gods and goddesses who lived on Mount Olympus and who intervened in the affairs of mortals. They were believed to come down to earth, in various disguises or even as animals. The idea was that a god or goddess could be anyone or anything,

so you'd better be on your best behaviour! The gods were
believed to be immortal and possessed of incredible power,
but they were also subject to human-like emotions and
passions. One of the most important gods in the Greek
pantheon was Zeus, the king of the gods. He was god of
the sky, lightning, thunder and law and order, who reigned
over Mount Olympus. Other major gods and goddesses included Poseidon, the god of the sea; Demeter, the goddess
of agriculture, and Athena, the goddess of wisdom and war.
Our goddess Artemis was twin sister to Apollo, who was
god of many things, such as music, prophesy and healing.

The Greeks believed that the gods had to be worshipped
and appeased through sacrifices and other rituals. These
rituals could take many forms, including the offering of animals, the burning of incense and the recitation of prayers.
Temples were built in honour of the gods, and festivals were
held to celebrate them. In addition to the major gods and
goddesses, the Greeks also believed in a number of lesser
gods and spirits who were associated with specific places
or activities. For example, Pan was the god of the wild, and
the nymphs were spirits associated with nature. The Greeks
also believed in oracles: there were holy sites where people
could go to seek guidance and advice from the gods. The
most famous oracle in Greece was the Oracle of Delphi,
which was believed to be the mouthpiece of the god Apollo.
Greek religion was also closely tied to Greek mythology – a
collection of stories and legends about the gods and their interactions with mortals. These myths provided the Greeks

with a framework for understanding the world around them and for exploring complex ethical questions.

Artemis was a significant goddess in Ancient Greek religion across Greece, with her cult centring around the city of Ephesus. Ephesus is actually on the western coast of Turkey, but in the classical period, it came under Greek influence as part of a league of cities called the Ionian League. The Temple of Artemis in Ephesus was considered one of the Seven Wonders of the Ancient World, and it served as a major pilgrimage site for worshippers of Artemis from all over the Mediterranean world. The temple was built around 550 BCE, but it was destroyed and rebuilt several times over the centuries. In fact, Pliny, the Roman statesman, tells us that the structure took 120 years to build. This final version of the temple was completed by the Roman Empire, and it was one of the largest temples in the ancient world. Sadly, only one of the columns remains today, and we know very little of the details of cultic worship here. It isn't entirely clear how the rituals would have been performed. The wider site of Ephesus is huge, with many different amenities, like baths, a library and aqueducts, which shows how many people it would need to serve. The theatre, for example, would hold around 25,000 spectators, possibly making it the largest in the ancient world. The cult of Artemis was not limited to Ephesus, however. There were numerous other sanctuaries and cult centres dedicated to her across the ancient Mediterranean world, from France and Spain in the west to Turkey and

Jordan in the east. Men may have been involved in her worship, especially if it conflated with other deities like her twin brother Apollo, but evidence strongly suggests that her cults were largely a female space.

The cult of Artemis was significant shaping the role of women in Ancient Greek society. Artemis was considered a symbol of female empowerment and independence, and her cult provided a space for women to gather, worship and celebrate their femininity. She often appeared in iconography as a young maiden, wearing short skirts to demonstrate her physical prowess, and carrying a bow and quiver. She is occasionally depicted in a natural setting or with animals next to her. Her punishments of those that cross her is well documented in myth, symbolic of the harsh realities of her wilderness, the place she is usually found roaming. She was a multifaceted divinity, a goddess of hunting, wilderness, childbirth, virginity and the moon.

The cult of Artemis offered women a level of agency and autonomy that was not available to them in other aspects of their lives. As we have seen, women were often excluded from political and economic life, and their roles were primarily limited to the domestic sphere. However, through the cult of Artemis, women were able to assert their own identities and take on leadership roles within the religious community. Women were involved in every aspect of the cult, from performing rituals and making offerings to serving as priestesses and even leading the worship of the goddess.

One of the most important aspects of the cult of Artemis was its emphasis on female purity and chastity. Artemis herself was prized for her virginity, and her worship was closely tied to the ideal of the virtuous woman. Young girls were often initiated into the cult of Artemis as part of their coming-of-age rituals and were taught to embody the ideals of purity and self-reliance. In addition to providing a space for women to gather and celebrate their femininity, the cult of Artemis also played an important role in women's health and well-being. Artemis was worshipped as a goddess of childbirth, and there was a range of rituals and practices designed to ensure the health and safety of mothers and their children. Women who were experiencing difficulties in childbirth turned to Artemis for protection and guidance, and her cult provided a supportive community of women who could offer practical and emotional support. As a goddess of the wilderness, she symbolised the ever-changing landscape, a place always in transition, never static. For women, whose bodies change regularly, first in puberty, then in pregnancy and childbirth, her wildness spoke deeply to them. At this place of borders, women could explore this, embraced by the goddess. There are so many reasons, therefore, that you might wish to worship this goddess.

The Greek travel writer Pausanias recorded the many festivals in Artemis's honour. The festivals were often observed annually in various parts of the ancient world, including Greece, Rome and Asia Minor, and were marked by a variety of rituals and ceremonies that honoured the goddess. These festivals varied greatly: each city-state would worship her with their own flair, according to their specific cultural vibes. In Brauron, a settlement not far from Athens, there was a popular festival held called the *Brauronia*. It was a coming-of-age celebration for young girls transitioning into womanhood. Allow me to transport you there ... But before I do, recall what the lives of women were like. I acknowledge the differences across locations, but in general, keep in mind the patriarchal context. Remember the daily lives of women; the lack of freedom and expression that was likely their reality.

You are around ten years old, and on the brink of puberty. You are used to visiting the temple and may have gone through several stages of initiation before the final one. You have been preparing for this event your whole life, cultivating your connection to Artemis by dancing for her, whispering to her, asking for her guidance and protection. You would have been told the mythical tale of ill-fated Iphigenia, Agamemnon's daughter. There are different versions of this story, but a brief outline tells us that during the Trojan War, two Athenian men killed a bear sacred to Artemis, so she sent a plague to punish them. In order to stop this, they needed a human sacrifice of a daughter to appease her. Iphigenia is given in sacrifice. Back now to the action. You may have been specifically chosen, selected as a representative of your community to take part in the ritual. You will make some offerings, perhaps a spindle or a piece of precious clothing. But the best bit is where you get wild, where you plug in directly to Artemis's sense of wildness and your own profound connection to nature. In the *arkteia*, you dress as a bear, a motif in many an Artemis myth and an embodiment of the wild. You dance slowly, as if to imitate the bear, wearing a short yellow *chiton* dress said to mimic the bear's skin, which you shed at the end to show you have matured and are ready to leave your childhood in the past. You emerge, prepared for womanhood, closer to Artemis.

So, in some ways, our goddess changed the world. The widespread popularity of her cult gave women a space to be themselves, to break free from the patriarchal shackles of Greek society. It gave them a chance to come together, unsupervised by men, and celebrate all aspects of their femininity. She also revealed to them the potential of femininity, beyond of the confines of a male perception. Artemis was brave, powerful, adventurous and unpredictable, just like the wild that she presided over. This is not to say Greek women shared the same privileges – society did not allow them to – but in her cult, they could explore these ideas, worship these qualities and come together to see what femininity could mean for them. The way Artemis punishes Actaeon, her vengeance, goes to show how seriously she took her own chastity.

In many ways, Artemis embodied a sense of wholeness and completeness that transcended traditional gender roles and expectations. She was seen as a goddess who encompassed both masculine and feminine qualities, representing a balance of strength and compassion, independence and nurturing. Her utter immersion in the wild, as goddess of nature, is an oppourtunity to reflect on the way we live today. In a fast-paced modern world where humans are increasingly detached from the nature, we suffer from increasing anxiety and a feeling of disconnectedness. As women, our deep relationship with nature is, to me, one that is even more sacred. For nature creates life and so do we. A reclaiming of Artemis is therefore a reminder not to forget the wild around us, its magical powers, its unique ability to ground us and embrace us. Artemis reminds us to take up our stewardship of this wonderful planet and lead the way. Be more Greta Thunberg!

It's not just the wild outside of us, however – we can also learn to embrace the wildness of our internal worlds, too. Which aspects of yourself do you deny because they are too wild or rough or too much? How many times have you diminished a feeling? Wanted to scream out into the void? To rage, sob and stamp until you are heard? All of these are the wild within, and I reckon it's just about time we let it all out.

RANGDA

Balinese Goddess of Evil, Black Magic and Balance

Rangda

Balinese Goddess of Evil,
Black Magic and Balance

The Widow

It was never easy for me; from the start. I was an outsider.
I was Javanese. I was ... well ... *other*. That otherness I
wore like a scent, swirling around me everywhere I went,
slick on my skin. It was a sickly fragrance, cloying, over-
powering. And no matter how much I washed, scrubbed at
it, masked it with other scents, it was always there. Sitting
in my nostrils, a constant reminder that I was different. I
saw it in the eyes of the community, too, how they caught
a whiff, how their eyes turned upwards to look at me and
their noses turned with them. I saw what they felt: a heavy
concoction of disgust laced with fear. That is a dangerous
combination; a deadly elixir just waiting for that first sip.
The only thing that kept me connected to these people

was dangling on the thinnest of threads. I was their Queen, reluctantly accepted, yet I had the protection and respect of my crown. That was, until I didn't . . .

I shake myself out of my memories and refocus on what I am doing. I now live an isolated life of exile deep in the Balinese jungle. Made to live alone due to my magic, mis-understood as dark, yet much more benevolent than they thought. I lie under my bamboo roof and listen to the wild sounds of the jungle at night and realise my outer environment mimics my inner world. The squawking, screeching and wailing I often hear is like the sound of my own soul, tormented, the physical pain announcing its presence. It taunts me, and with every dreaded night I sink deeper and deeper into my isolation and the hatred hardens within me, a stone in place of a heart that used to be full of light. My insides become blacker day by day, my soul collapses in on itself under the pressure and intensity of my dark emotions.

I look down at my pot and snap off the bat's wing I procured this morning, arrow sharp, hand steady. I toss it into the vat and mumble words of the darkest magic I can muster. My anger boils along with the potion, until something in me stirs. I sense a presence in the jungle, discernible only by the faintest rustle. Someone is here. I peer out of my hut. 'Who dares approach me?' I bellow into the dense tropical trees. 'Please, Queen Mahendradatta, I come with news from your son, King Airlangga, do not hurt me!'

He appears from the bushes, shaking in fear and avoiding

my eyes. It is clear to me he will not even enter my clearing, preferring to cling to the edges of the jungle. Little does he know that physical barriers mean nothing to a witch. And then it dawns on me, the words he has used. My reply comes swift and fast: 'What do you mean my son, the king?' He tentatively steps into the clearing and into the moonlight. I see him now. Only a boy, with sweat beading on his forehead, meandering down the sides of his face and onto his bare, hairless chest. His skin is flawless, waxy smooth and a beautiful shade of a rich medium brown. I realise how much I miss people; and then the pain of exile stabs in the middle of my chest, knocking the air from my lungs. I take a deep, slow and conscious breath to steady myself. 'I am sorry, my Queen, but your husband is dead, so your son is now king and you are now *Rangda*, a widow.'

The news hits me so hard that for the first time in my life, I freeze. As I stand barefoot in my hut, everything slows down and I can feel every ounce of energy in the moment. I feel the hot, sticky breeze against my supple skin; my heart beating in my ears; the black hairs on my arms standing on end, and every single muscle in my body tense in anticipation for what will come next. It is as though even the jungle has finally stopped its deafening taunt of me, as everything falls silent awaiting my action. Tall palms reach high into the deep-blue sky, mingling with the humid mists. Every shade of green is around me, interspersed with the soft pink petals of the frangipani, its scent so pleasant, and for a moment I forget myself. Then an unfamiliar feeling rises in me. At first, I am afraid of it, and resist its presence. But then I get curious, and sink deeper into it, watching it carefully to see what it is. It is so foreign to me that it takes a good few minutes to work out what it is. A tear forms in my eye as I recognise that old friend, lost to dark times, lost to loneliness, lost to betrayal and heartache. I see you. And you are called hope.

The boy coughs, my mind snaps back to the scene. I soften and even smile. The boy now looks confused and worried, as I notice his hand move to the handle of the knife at his side. 'Do not fear me, boy,' I say. 'I wish you no harm. When will my son, the king, come? Has he commanded me back to him? What message does he send for me?' Behind all of these words is a feeling that I haven't had for years; love is filling the cavernous dark hole that has been my heart for so long.

My exile is over. It was my husband who stripped me bare in humiliation, snatched away my remedies, in utter revulsion of the magic that had become my life. I was a healer, not a witch. When I arrived from Java, I was homesick. I roamed the jungle and learned all about the plants and herbs I found, some the same as in my homeland and others new. They became my purpose and I had hoped to use my skills to ingratiate myself with the people, to help them. But witchcraft was called. They vilified me, called me a sorceress and worse, still, accused me of black magic. Life is funny, isn't it? The darkness they put inside me with their cruel actions was the seed for my black magic. They birthed what I am. And now I fix my gaze back on the boy, who has an expression I know only too well: utter terror.

He turns to flee, all arms and legs, but manages to squeeze some words in-between his heavy breaths as he runs. The words he speaks are the beginning of the end: 'The. Exile. Remains.' He disappears behind dark green palms as I fall to my knees and scream the scream of the worst type of despair you can imagine. As I look up into the night sky, I watch as all the remnants of hope, love and light leave my body. I observe them as they sail into the blackness of the night sky, away, far away, never to return . . .

And then I summon them, the most terrifying creatures known to man: the *Leyaks*. Demonic creatures, disgusting heads that fly with entrails hanging loose, they devour new-born children or those yet unborn. They can shapeshift, appear as normal humans by daylight, or even an innocent-looking pig, all the while hiding their truly horrific nature within. It is still night, and I see them flying towards me over the canopy of the lush trees, entrails of heart, liver and bowel hanging beneath them as they brush the tops of the trees, leaving bloody stains. I see their fangs protruding, eyes bulging and long, slimy tongues. Their eyes are fixed forward as they soar over my head and, by my command, head for the community.

There is no going back now; the power I have released is unrelenting. This is the end of them. I smile a crooked smile, anger bubbling in my heart. I cannot wait to watch them suffer, behold my dark powers and bow down in front of them. I will break them as they have broken me. Sweet son, how you have forsaken me. And then, the screams, those bloodcurdling screams of real terror, and I run, I run towards them to watch from the darkness of the forest as blackness descends upon them.

I see a young woman clutching her husband who has fallen foul of some disgusting disease, covered in boils and panting his last breaths. Victims of my rage and dark magic. She is screaming and stroking his head, pleading for help, for someone, for anyone to help him. A child, a young girl, runs to her side with a cup of water and places it to her father's mouth. As his gingerly sips, life slips away from him. I feel conflicted as I watch, for I was once a healer and could save this man with only a few words and a sprinkle of herbs. But they have made me this, torn between the two worlds within me, torn between doing good and doing bad. I am their creation, and they must live with it. I withdraw just as the man's soul leaves his body as *karma* takes over, his fate sealed, his soul ready for whatever is next for it.

The next day, I awaken to the sound of men. Many men. They are close but not yet in my clearing. I hear their feet as they crunch over the detritus of the jungle floor, subtle to the average ears but not for someone with my power. I peer out of my hut through the gaps in the bamboo. I see one, fully armed, his dagger at his side – the *Keris* – eyes darting left and right. I can smell the fear emanating from him.

It is almost dawn, the sky turning from a silky blue to a light pink, like the petals of a lotus flower. Wispy clouds crawl across the sky, as the sun rises and lights them from behind. I realise I must act quickly as the men are closing in on me. I shut my eyes and begin the incantations, only to be interrupted by a single male voice, one I recognise.

'Mother,' he says. 'Mother, please do not do that. Please listen to what I have to say.' I force my eyes open and bring myself to meet his. He stands there at the entrance of my hut, in all of his regal finery. Yet I cannot help but notice he is in his battle attire and the fact that he has come dressed like this is more wounding than the Keris he carries at his side. He means me harm. His eyes, like deep pools of mud, are fixed upon me, filled with a heavy concoction of fear, hope and love – an unholy trinity. I observe his pulse beating hard in his neck, and then his soft dark golden skin, the skin I used to stroke to ease him to sleep. Forcing down the years of unwept tears is hard, but I know I must show him none of my deep grief at losing him. I answer him with one word: 'Speak.'

He sits down on the floor with a heavy thud and begins. 'Mother, I come here to plead with you to stop. The Leyaks are wreaking havoc on my people; many are dying of awful diseases. Mothers, husbands, children – all in agony with the curse you have unleashed upon us. Why? Why have you done this?'

I snort in disgust. 'You mean you really do not know why? Look around you, son. You abandoned me. Left me here to rot. *You* made me into this.' I realise I am now crying – no not crying, sobbing. Those deep sobs that emerge when you release the pressure valve that contains the pain. Just a little turn, as without that pain who will I even be?

Airlangga looks agitated now, as if this has taken him by surprise. 'But Mother, you chose black magic over me. Over us all. And now as king, I must act. What you have become . . . I do not recognise her. If you do not retract the curse, I will take action.'

He rises to his feet, and I see the strong man he has become. He is towering over me, muscles tense and firm, and I notice his hand hovering over his Keris, poised to attack. He learns forward, towards my left ear, and whispers a poison into it that is the death of me all over again: 'You are dead to me, Mother. And now I must destroy you.'

He turns and runs out of the hut, and I am left bereft, permanently locked into the darkness of my soul, with only pain and sorrow for company. So be it. I step into the clearing. I raise my arms and eyes to the skies, summon the Leyaks and begin the work. The work of evil.

The battle that ensues is bloody and vile. Men are torn to shreds by the Leyaks as they feast on the flesh of the wounded and, worse still, on the dead. They try in vain to protect themselves, slashing away with their daggers, but how can you kill something that is not alive? They fall. And fast.

I watch all of this as if in slow motion, in a sort of dissociated state. Neither present nor absent, completely devoid of any emotion. I am empty. My thoughts are abruptly interrupted by a sound so faint that only a witch could discern it. A quiet incantation, at the edge of the jungle. I feel the panic rising as I hone in on the words being uttered, only to realise they are the words of my son. And in further horror, I realise he is summoning the only thing that can stop me. My opposite. The great Barong. Commander of the spirits of good, the mighty power of the light. I know I must act fast before he comes, for when he does it is over for me. I mutter the words of the worst spell I can imagine and open my eyes to see it taking hold. The Leyaks have now stopped and float about the men as if time has been suspended. The men all stand, entranced, and face me. Eyes fixed on me, wearing blank expressions as those who have been hypnotised often do. I lift my arm in commandment, and each man places his hand on his Keris. Airlangga rushes in front of me, the only one I have not allowed this horror to be inflicted upon. Despite his betrayal, I still cannot bring myself to destroy my own son. He drops to his knees in front on me, eyes full of tears, and I am transported back to a time when he was young. I want to sweep him up in my arms, console him, hush him to a deep and restful sleep. But no. I will not stop. I cannot. This is how it is now. I look ahead, all of the men ready for my final command. Airlangga follows my gaze as I mutter the words. As soon as I do, his men snatch up their kerises and I command them to plunge them straight into their stomachs. I shut my eyes because a scene like that is too horrific even for me to watch.

When I open my eyes, Airlangga is before me. But it

is not him who I am looking at. Standing beside him is the great jungle cat, Barong. His lion-like mane is made of thick white fur, surrounding his red head and bulging red eyes, fangs hanging out of his mouth. He is gilded in jewellery and mirrors. As I stare at him, directly into his eyes, I am, for the first time, deeply fearful. My heart beats loudly in my ears as I sense the terror that is surely to come. Behind Barong, all of the men are alive. He must have cast his own spell to save them. The Leyaks have fled. And there is only me.

With a roar, Barong leaps towards me and I know I must run. I pound through the jungle with him hot on my heels; as I weave through the dense trees looking for places to hide. I know this is the end; there is no spell I can cast that will work. We are doomed to this fate for ever, me running further and further into my darkness and Barong chasing me with the light of the good. Locked in an eternal dance.

I slip into the undergrowth and find a moment of shelter. I collapse in utter exhaustion. Slipping into unconsciousness, I see only him, my boy, Airlangga's face, as the darkness engulfs me and makes me its servant. For Mahendradatta is dead. Now there is only Rangda.

Rangda's World

When you conjure up an image of Bali, you probably think of beautiful sandy beaches, lush green forests and spiritual retreats. Forgive the cliché, but I think of Julia Roberts in

Eat, Pray, Love, a favourite film of mine, mainly because I get to see so much of Bali in it, a place full of wonder and amazement for me. Maybe my obsession is about how 'otherworldly' Bali seems for a girl who grew up in a council estate in East London. I have been fortunate enough to travel the world, but I have still not managed to get to Bali – I think I am saving it for something really special.

Because my brain is obsessed with the ancient past, I decided to live vicariously through it and look into historic Balinese goddesses, and I found an absolute cracker in Rangda. There are many variants in the origins of her story, and my retelling is based on just one, the tale of a real-life, eleventh-century Javanese princess Mahendradatta. Some have argued that the origin of the Rangda story comes from this princess, who upon her arrival from neighbouring Java, became Queen of Bali. She was also mother to Balinese hero and king, Airlangga. Possibly because of her devotion to the Hindu goddess Durga (in fact, she may have brought the cult to Bali), she was closely associated with her. Durga is a formidable goddess, of protection, strength and destruction. Therefore, later depictions of Mahendradatta became synonymous with Durga, and it is also believed that Durga is one of the inspiring figures behind Rangda's tale.

The source material for these stories is hard to determine, but the tales emerge from a mixture of theatrical Balinese dance performances, called *Topeng*, in which the Balinese tell well-known tales of heroes, kings and myths accompanied by traditional musical instruments and dressed in elaborate costumes. We also have some other sources, such as palm leaf manuscripts, as well as manuscripts that outline certain historical events. In this retelling, I have merged all of these legendary aspects to create my personal take of Rangda's story. So come with me as we delve into a Bali not defined by its tourism, but rather by its wonderfully rich cultural history.

Speaking of that history, it can be a little hard to pin things down. Both the archaeological and historical records are incomplete, leaving gaps in our knowledge. Then we have the issue of the rapidly changing landscape, be it through volcanic activity or the fast-growing dense jungle, which engulf archaeological finds, confusing the evidence further. We do have some wonderful pieces, however, such as the rich cultural history that has been passed down in the manuscripts known as *Iontar*, which inscribe religious, philosophical and poetic ideas onto palmyra palms. Another issue is that there is not a prolific amount of academic scholarship, possibly owing to the difficulties faced with lack of evidence.

But enough of what we don't have – more of what we do! Balinese people have retained a close relationship to their cultural traditions and continue to practise them to this day, passed down by generations. Through their ritualistic practices, community philosophies, religious beliefs and cultural connections, we can access historic Bali through the people themselves. Much of what I refer to as 'historic' Bali might be relevant for modern Bali as well, and we must acknowledge that the generalisation of the term 'historic' is not ideal. However, it will allow for a base from which to jump off into the world of Bali's rich past, so I am going to let that one slide.

So what of historic Bali? What would life have been like for the earlier inhabitants of this beautiful Island? Bali's history is a tapestry woven with various influences, primarily shaped by Hinduism, which arrived on the island around the first century CE. In fact, Indonesia is the largest Muslim nation in the world. Bali, however, is an exception to this rule, as about 87 per cent of its people identify as Hindu. Hinduism in Bali is a unique combination of traditional Hindu beliefs alongside indigenous customs that pre-date the arrival of Hinduism. The integration of indigenous beliefs with Hindu practices resulted in the birth of a distinct Balinese Hinduism, characterised by intricate rituals, elaborate ceremonies and sacred temples. Temples played a central role in ancient Balinese society. These architectural marvels were not only places of worship but also cultural and community centres. The temples were adorned with ornate carvings, intricately designed gates and towering pagodas. *Pura Besakih*, built on the slopes of the volcano Mount Agung in eastern Bali, was likely founded as a holy site in prehistoric times and it remains a significant spiritual site to this day. The temple complex of *Pura Taman Ayun*, with its stunning gardens and moats, is another architectural gem that provides a glimpse into historic Bali's grandeur. Religious ceremonies and festivals formed an integral part of Balinese life, both at these temples and within communities and homes. These vibrant celebrations brought communities together and showcased their devotion to the gods. The natural beauty of the island captivated its inhabitants and inspired their artistic expressions – art and creativity flourished in historic Bali. Skilled artisans crafted intricate wood carvings, vibrant paintings and delicate textiles. The art was often imbued with mythological themes and stories, reflecting the spiritual and cultural beliefs of the Balinese people. This artistic tradition continues to thrive in modern Bali, making it a hub for creative endeavours and a paradise for art enthusiasts. The mask of Rangda is a popular choice for those seeking a souvenir to take home from Bali, but the Balinese have their own sacred masks which are kept safely within communities, separate to those sold for commercial purposes. The mask of Rangda is a sacred object of worship that is usually kept in a temple and has protective associations. The masks are taken out to perform in ceremonies at important events like the Barong Dance. Its bulbous eyes with red circles, large teeth and protruding bright red tongue are no doubt to exaggerate the monstrous nature of the character of Rangda. The people of Bali believe that these masks allow the performer to transform into the character they are portraying. Many dancers will even sleep with their mask beside them, so they can understand its true character. More than this, performers essentially become a conduit for the spirit they portray, making the ritual dances so much more than entertainment – they are a deeply spiritual experiment for those that partake in them.

Where there is now a central government of Indonesia overseeing the governance of Bali, historically it was ruled by kings and queens. Many of these ruling elites came from neighbouring territories and we must acknowledge the external influences these nations had on Bali, politically, historically and of course culturally. Maritime trade brought contact with neighbouring civilisations, including India, China and various South East Asian kingdoms. The cultural exchanges enriched Bali's heritage, leaving traces in its architecture, arts and cuisine. The island also faced occasional conflicts and invasions, shaping its history and resilience. This is perhaps what makes Bali so interesting – the blending of cultures in this one island produce something that is distinctive and unique.

The social fabric of Bali revolved around the concept of community (*Banjar*). Villages were divided into smaller units, each with its own temple and communal meeting hall. The Banjar system fostered a strong sense of unity and cooperation among the Balinese people, which is still prevalent in the island's society today and may have more ancient origins. The Balinese community, with its rich cultural and historical background, is guided by several important concepts that have shaped their way of life for centuries. These concepts have deep roots in Bali's history and reflect the island's unique blend of indigenous, Hindu and other cultural influences. The community is guided by several important concepts that shape their way of life. *Tri Hita Karana* (three causes/ways to happiness or harmony) is a fundamental Balinese spiritual principle that highlights the need for balance and harmony between humans, the divine and the natural environment. The concept of *Desa, Kala, Patra* (the place, the time and the object) emphasises the importance of context, appropriate timing and suitable places in conducting various activities. *Gotong Royong* (carrying a burden upon the shoulders together/ collectively), the spirit of cooperation and communal work, encourages Balinese people to come together, support one another and contribute to the collective well-being. Finally, the concept of *Bhinneka Tunggal Ika* – It is different, yet it is one – is the official national motto of Indonesia and is usually translated as: 'Unity in Diversity'. This reflects the Balinese acceptance and celebration of religious and cultural diversity on the island. These concepts shape the Balinese values, behaviours and interactions, fostering a sense of belonging, cooperation and respect among its members.

Let us look at those members for a moment. Balinese society has long been characterised by distinct gender roles. Historically, men and women occupied different spheres of influence and responsibility. Men were primarily engaged in agricultural activities, trade and governance, while women focused on domestic duties, child-rearing and community support. The societal structure was patriarchal, with men holding dominant positions in decision-making processes, inheritance and property ownership. It must be noted that this patriarchy has often been used as a method of suppression for Balinese women. The impact of this is that women have been subordinated by male dominance under the guise of religious belief. As a result Balinese women are often constricted into traditional gender-defined roles, such as the wife or the mother, and this has had a profound effect on the rights of women in Bali. This is not to say that in the private worship of their Hindu gods and goddesses Balinese women do not find their own personal methods of expression through religious practice. It is quite possible that through the worship of figures like Rangda, Balinese women are able to explore aspects of their character that may be supressed in the mainstream religion. As such, it could be that religion may be one of the only places where women can express themselves. Although the laws are changing in Bali to move towards a more equitable society, it must be said that there is a long way to go before Balinese women gain an equal position in legal and social terms.

What do we know of earlier Balinese culture? Did women have a more active role in society? One space in which women excelled was dance. They dedicated themselves to mastering traditional dance forms like *Legong* and *Barong*, using graceful movements to express mythological stories. The meticulous training and skill required in these dances allowed them to showcase their talent and contribute to the vibrant cultural fabric of Bali. Interestingly, the role of Rangda was often taken up by a male performer, perhaps in further subversion of feminine power. Additionally, women's proficiency in playing the *Gamelan*, the traditional musical ensemble, enriched the cultural performances and brought joy to those who experienced them. In their agrarian society, Balinese women actively participated in rice cultivation alongside the men. From planting to harvesting and processing, they shared in the labour that sustained their livelihood. The cooperative nature of their society allowed them to contribute to the success of their agricultural endeavours, fostering a deep sense of belonging and unity. While their roles were primarily within the domestic and community spheres, there were instances where women could attain positions of power and influence.

Like many ancient cultures around the world, the responsibility for healing and curing was the woman's domain, with their deep and respected knowledge of local herbs, natural remedies and physical treatments. As societies progressed and external cultural influences infiltrated Bali, especially through Western colonialists like the Dutch who brought Christian ideals, healing was conflated with magic and magic with darkness. Those who practised anything remotely like it were seen as in league with the Devil, and this aspect of feminine power was relentlessly eradicated. As is all too often the case, the demonisation of women who held holistic knowledge, or magical knowledge, led to accusations of witchcraft. We are well aware of the horrendous impact that this had on women in the west, and despite the lack of specific evidence of this in Bali, we might imagine some similar issues, especially in more urbanised areas. However, in rural areas, people held on to their traditions and today Bali remains a place of natural and herbal treatments and remedies.

How else might women wield power in historic Bali? Though rare, women from noble families were able to ascend to the positions of queens or regents, exerting authority and actively participating in decision-making processes. Within the cultural and religious framework of Bali, they found a sense of agency and respect. Their lives were shaped by a deep devotion to their religious beliefs, the pursuit of artistic expression and active engagement in agricultural activities.

And so to Rangda. Is she the evil demonic witch or is there something more significant at play? The worship of Rangda is a fascinating and intricate aspect of Balinese religious and cultural practices. Some scholars suggest that it has its roots in pre-Hindu indigenous beliefs and practices. While archaeological findings are limited in the context of religious rituals and beliefs, they do contribute to our understanding of the ancient traditions associated with Rangda worship. Excavations have revealed the remnants of temple structures and sculptures that may be associated with Rangda. For example, the archaeological site of *Goa Gajah*, or the Elephant Cave, located near Ubud, Bali, may have had associations with our goddess. The cave complex features intricate carvings depicting mythological figures, including a possible figure of Rangda herself. Outside of this, it is tough to be certain about the ritual relationships the Balinese had with Rangda historically, and so we generally rely on the strong oral tradition for our evidence.

Bali's indigenous traditions likely revered female deities associated with fertility, protection and spiritual power. Over time, as Hinduism became dominant in Bali, the existing belief systems merged and adapted to incorporate Hindu deities and mythologies. Some scholars have argued that she is often conflated with the Hindu goddesses Durga and Kali, who share some of her destructive powers. What is perhaps more likely is that the tales of Rangda, like many of our goddesses, have undergone many revisions and additions to create a rich cultural canon. As such, she likely contains elements from indigenous, Hindu and other cultures.

Rangda is often depicted with wild hair, bulging eyes, fangs and claw-like nails, creating a frightening image that symbolises her power. Therefore, one cannot deny that she is an intimidating figure who on the surface is as she seems: a terrifying force to be reckoned with. In Balinese mythology and folklore, Rangda is referred to as a deity or a supernatural entity rather than specifically being labelled as a goddess. She exists in a kind of grey area between the supernatural, primeval, symbolic and godly. She is a powerful figure associated with dark forces, chaos and the supernatural realm. Rangda is considered the queen or the personification of Leyaks, malevolent spirits associated with black magic and witchcraft. Leyaks are believed to be servants of Rangda, carrying out her bidding and causing harm to humans. The worship and reverence of Rangda highlight the Balinese belief in the existence of powerful supernatural forces and their desire to maintain balance and harmony between opposing energies. Balinese Hindus believe that the universe is comprised of a delicate equilibrium between positive and negative energies, and the worship of Rangda serves as a means to maintain this balance. It is important to understand that the worship of Rangda is not an endorsement of evil or darkness, but rather an acknowledgement of its existence and an attempt to mitigate its effects. Balinese Hindus seek protection from Rangda's negative energies through their devotion to the gods, participation in rituals and adherence to religious customs. Therefore, if we really want to get to know Rangda, we need to look beneath the surface of the monstrous and consider her layers. Underneath a fearsome casing which is by no mean insignificant – lies a deep-seated need to balance energies in an attempt to calm the choppy waters that are the human existence. When we relegate her to the evil witch, we deny the deep truths she hides within her.

The people of Bali seek to appease Rangda through ritualistic dances and performances. The Barong and Rangda dance is a dramatic representation of the eternal struggle between good and evil, with Rangda embodying the destructive forces that need to be overcome. The dance involves intricate choreography, ornate costumes and elaborate masks to portray the fierce and supernatural nature of Rangda. As has been outlined above, it is important to note that the worship of Rangda does not involve adoration or reverence, but rather seeks to neutralise her negative energies and protect against her malevolent influences. The aim is to maintain balance and harmony in the cosmic order. During specific rituals, offerings are made to appease Rangda and prevent her from causing harm. These offerings typically consist of food, flowers, incense and symbolic objects that are believed to redirect Rangda's destructive energy. In addition to the religious rituals, Rangda also holds a place in traditional healing practices. Some healers, known as *Balian* or traditional medicine practictioners, channel the power of Rangda to counteract negative spiritual influences and restore health and well-being to patients. There are many practising Balians; in fact, some say there are more Balians than there are medical doctors. A Balian can be either male or female and will use magic, herbs, oils, massage and other methods to address issues in the body.

It is also important for us to explore what Rangda meant (and continues to mean) to the women of Bali. We must note that the significance of Rangda's worship can vary among different social classes, regions and individual beliefs. Balinese society is diverse, and the role of Rangda in the lives of women would have been shaped by local customs and practices. Nonetheless, the worship of Rangda provides women with avenues for empowerment, expression and spiritual connection, contributing to their sense of identity, agency and belonging within the cultural and religious fabric of the community. Therefore, my suggestions are meant for consideration; I am not prescribing what an individual Balinese woman chooses to take from the Rangda story herself. I will also frame this in the context of historic Bali, as much of our discussion has centred around this.

In a patriarchal society, where women often faced societal restrictions and gender-based inequalities, Rangda's image as a strong and independent figure could have served as a source of inspiration. Her depiction as a witch and her association with dark forces might have challenged conventional notions of femininity and provided a platform for women to explore alternative expressions of power. Perhaps it allowed women to reconcile the darkness within them. Additionally, in the religious context, Rangda's worship would have allowed women to engage with the spiritual realm on their own terms. Balinese religious rituals, including those associated with Rangda, often involved active participation, where individuals would make offerings, recite prayers and engage in various ceremonial practices. Women, alongside men, would have experienced a sense of connection and communion with the divine. This would in turn have empowered women in a society where the female voice was perhaps not permitted to be as loud.

As we explored in the retelling at the beginning of this chapter, Rangda is much more than an evil force. Her role as a protective deity would have been significant for Balinese women. Society placed great importance on the well-being and safety of the family, and women, as caretakers, would have sought divine intervention and protection for themselves and their loved ones. The tale of Rangda, with its focus on balancing negative forces and seeking harmony, would have provided a sense of security and assurance to women in navigating the challenges and uncertainties of life. Moreover, the representation of Rangda as the queen of Leyaks, and her ability to control them, may have invoked a sense of control and mastery over the unseen forces that pose threats to individuals and communities. Women might have sought Rangda's guidance and invoked her protection against malevolent influences, particularly in the context of childbirth, where the safety of both mother and child was of paramount importance.

Rangda has a lot to tell us. Patriarchy has damned her to be a single-faceted figure, to be feared, to be repressed, to be a reminder of the dangers of giving a woman power and how she may misuse it. Her story can speak to the anger felt by women in a society ruled by men – a metaphorical exploration of the repressed woman. But I do not see just that, and neither should you. What I see is a figure that is key in balancing life, a holistic image, neither good nor bad, but both at the same time. Rangda is a much-needed spirit in Balinese thinking, an essential aspect of life on earth. Without her, chaos ensues. What Rangda really is, if you dig deep enough, is a great stabilising force. Much like the concept of Yin and Yang, she demands her rightful place. Ignore her, and you become out of balance, out of sync with the world around you. Far from the idea of an evil witch that should be suppressed, Rangda's rage bubbles up to ask you to pay attention.

Think of the times that your balance is out of whack. Do you notice rage coming along for the ride? I certainly do. When my dualistic aspects of self – my light and my dark, my feminine and my masculine, my doing and my being or my Rangda and my Barong – are off kilter, I get tetchy. Tetchy turns to anger. And why does this happen? Because our inner energies are asking us to sit up and take note of what we are doing, which side of us needs attention, love and respect. It's no good only accepting the light sides of ourselves, the bits that we are happy to show off to the world. For the parts of us that we shove into the dark, force into exile, like our Rangda here, are bound to scream and shout until we listen. For all Rangda wants is to be seen and respected for what she is – a precious component of life itself. That dark is OK; that rage and anger are not only allowed, but a sacred part of our inner worlds. Supress a force that powerful at your peril. To deny this is to deny our own truth.

So, tell the world, femininity can be dark. It can be angry. Embrace it. Honour it. Next time the Rangda within rages, go to her and listen. Tell her that it is OK to step out of the shadows . . . Wear her with pride.

INANNA

Sumerian Goddess, Queen of Heaven and Earth, War and Sexuality

Inanna

*Sumerian Goddess, Queen of Heaven
and Earth, War and Sexuality*

The Descent

I am girl. I am goddess. I am Queen. Queen of all Heaven
and goddess of love, fertility, war and power. All of my
senses are on fire – sound first, as I listen to the sounds of
the Great Below. It is time.

I call upon my most faithful and kind *sukkal*, adviser.
She sweeps in, the scent of sweet jasmine floating around
her, jarring with the emotional weight of the atmosphere
in here. I fix my dark brown eyes on her and say, 'You
know what to do?' 'Yes, my Queen, I know the plan.' With
a single and slight nod of my head, we begin.

She places the *shugurra*, my crown, on my head, averting
her eyes from holding my gaze as she does so. I cannot be
sure, but I think I detect a tear forming in her eye. Next, she

arranges my long, silky black hair around the crown, and hooks my lapis beads around my neck, which nestle in the fold of my breasts. Finally, she drapes my heavy royal robes about my shoulders. 'Go now,' I command. She scuttles off. I need to finish this myself, steel myself with a moment of calm contemplation before I make my descent. I add my breastplate, my golden ring and snatch up my sceptre of power. I am Queen. I am ready.

We float down, slow and steady, caught in the soft breezes of the desert. Like a feather dancing with the wind, we glide. Down and down, deeper and deeper. Air becomes land, as we go under. To the Great Below.

The air is rancid, the light absent: this is a place where hope does not dwell. I turn to my adviser. 'Remember, if I do not return, go to my father Enki and ask for help.' She nods, and soars upwards, back to the Great Above. My home.

I stand tall and knock loudly at the gates of death. Neti, the gatekeeper, appears, and asks who knocks. I reply, 'I am Inanna, Queen of the Great Above. I come to see my sister, Ereshkigal, and witness the funeral rites of my brother-in-law, the Bull of Heaven.' He replies curtly, 'Wait.' The gate slams shut and I am left with my thoughts.

In the dark silence, I replay the events that have led me here. Rage boils inside me as I remember the insults of that braggart Gilgamesh. After he killed the demon Humbaba in the Cedar Forest, I caught sight of him. Freshly washed, adorned in royal robes – his godly power swelled the desire inside me. I wanted him; I felt the heat in-between my thighs. But he refused my advances, foolishly. He claimed that my many lovers had met bad ends, had suffered after laying with me. Ha! I am goddess. Sometimes a mortal cannot survive in the fires of my lust; it is simply too much for them. They burn, in some way or another. I decided he would burn anyway.

Bile rises in my mouth as I replay the offence in my mind. I called upon my father god and asked for vengeance. He refused, doubling the intensity of my anger. I convinced him to gift me the Bull of Heaven, so that I could bring chaos upon the world by using the Bull to smash open the Great Below and watch the dead pour out among the living. A way for me to release my fury and set a trap for Gilgamesh – punishing his terrible rejection of me. My father consented, and for a brief moment I watched in glee as the Bull ravaged the land, opening up cracks in the earth, into which men cascaded and fell, swallowed up. Gone.

But then Gilgamesh charged into my city, the great Uruk, with his companion Enkidu, and they fought the Bull. They prevailed. Enkidu crept up behind the Bull and pulled its tail while Gilgamesh thrust his sword into the Bull's neck. Now, I slam my fists against the gate of the Great Below as I feel the horror at what happened next coursing through my veins. I stood on the walls of Uruk, and damned them both. Enkidu threw the Bull's thigh at me in utter disrespect to my godliness. He had gone too far.

Soon, the gods sent to him a terrible plague. He screamed in agony until the very end. It was a just demise; one must never reach higher than the gods.

The gate creeks, and I am brought back to the present. Neti appears, a furtive look on his face. He fixes his eyes on me and says: 'Enter, Inanna, through this first gate.' I step forward, and as I do, my crown is swiftly removed from my head. I grasp Neti's wrist, with my *shugurra* still in his hand, and bore my eyes into him. 'What is the meaning of this insult?' I bellow. Neti's reply comes fast and hard, 'Quiet, Inanna. The ways of the underworld are perfect; they may not be questioned.' I sigh, realising that in my sister's domain, my power does not exist.

And so, we continue in this fashion, reaching each of the seven gates that are the entry to the underworld. At every gate, I am stripped of my powers more. I am no longer Queen. I feel like a girl. At the very last gate, Neti takes my royal robes, and I am naked. It is as though with every garment stolen, a piece of my godly soul has been removed. It is a curious feeling this, to feel almost mortal. Vulnerable. Weak. Exposed.

Mingled with this is a sense of foreboding and fear. I look down and notice my hands are trembling, a heady mix of anxiety and the cold, deathly breeze of the underworld. Neti prods my back. 'Go on then, enter.' I push open the final gate, knowing that *she* is on the other side, waiting.

As I step into the high-vaulted throne room of the dead, it is her rage and deep grief that I feel first. Swimming all over my naked body. Causing me to gasp in shock. I turn my eyes to the floor, afraid to meet her gaze.

Ereshkigal rises from her throne, sweeps across the stone-cold floor. She looms above me and says with words as cold as ice, 'Inanna, look at me.' Bowed low, I tear my eyes away from the floor and meet hers. The same dark brown glistening eyes; mine full of remorse, hers full of tears and pain. For a brief moment, we are just sisters. Two girls staring up through the mighty branches of the *huluppu* tree, in the hot summer sun, the light bending and refracting, pouring through the gaps in the branches like endless strings of precious gems. This tree is sacred, it connects my world and hers. The Above with the Below.

A tear falls from my eye, for I am now acutely aware of my fate. I know my sister well; I can read her intention with the intensity of her stare. My heart opens a crack, breaking off, a piece lost for ever. My only chance of redemption is now in the hands of my adviser. As the judges of the underworld swarm and surround me, damming me to death for what I have done, I hear Ereshkigal's damnation of my guilt, her spikey words of wrath. I even feel the back of her hand as it strikes my face, full force, the metallic taste of blood. I am here but not here; I feel my life force fading already. I slump forward, palms on the floor of the dead. I look at Ereshkigal one more time, my eyes swimming with pleas. Cold emptiness in hers. I raise my hand in supplication. But then, blackness . . .

*

The adviser is pacing. It has been three days and three nights; Inanna is still not home. She knows what to do. The great Queen commanded it. She gathers her belongings and sets off for Nippur and the temple of Enlil, the seat of the great god. She enters the holy space and cries out to the great father. Pleading with him to save his daughter, to force Ereshkigal to release Inanna from the underworld. The answer comes, a resounding, angry boom that bounces off the walls of the temple. 'My daughter craved the Great Above. She who is received into the underworld does not return. She who goes to the Dark City stays there.'

The adviser tries again, making the same plea to the god of the moon, Nanna. She receives the same answer.

For a third and final time, she tries Enki. He replies, 'What has happened? Inanna! Queen of All the Lands! Holy Priestess of Heaven! What has happened? I am troubled. I am grieved.' He reaches his mighty hand down into the earth and sweeps up dirt under his fingernail. With this, he fashions a *kurgarra*, an entity neither male nor female. He does this again, this time making a *galatur*, an entity that is also not male, not female. He gives the food of life to the kurgarra and the water of life to the galatur, telling them both what they must do. Like flies, they slip through the cracks of the gates to the depths of the underworld, until they reach its throne.

They find the Queen of the Great Below, Ereshkigal, moaning and writhing in the throes of childbirth. She screams in agony. The kurgarra and galatur do as Father

Enki commanded: they reply to the Queen's cries. As predicted by Enki, this pleases Ereshkigal, and she turns to them: 'As you sigh with me and feel my pain, I will give you a gift. A gift of water perhaps? Or a grain-gift?' 'We do not wish it,' they chime in unison. 'That is what we want, over there.' All eyes dart to what it is that they want. What they have made this dreaded journey for. What Inanna had planned and hoped for all along. They are looking at her: *Inanna*. At her rotten, naked corpse hanging like a piece of discarded meat from a hook on a wall.

Now, with the food and water of life brought by the kurgarra and galatur, I am revived. My eyes snap open, but even the dim light of the underworld is too much for them to bear. As I awaken, I get my bearings and realise the truth. My fears are confirmed – my sister took her revenge, took my life as penance for the life of her husband, The Bull of Heaven. Still, now, it is done. It is time to leave this behind.

I make my way to the throne-room gate, avoiding Ereshkigal's stare. I need to leave now. But hands clasp at my arms, dragging me back down. The Anunna, gods of the underworld, proclaim, 'You cannot leave, Inanna, not without someone taking your place.' Of course, it cannot be that easy. Death always asks for payment.

I take my leave, back through the seven gates of the Great Below, the *gallas*, demons of the underworld, clinging to my robes, weighing me down. They are pitiful creatures who know no food or drink, no offerings, no sweet lovemaking. Together we fly, up and up to the gates of my palace. There,

I see my beautiful adviser, who has saved me. She throws herself in the dust at my feet. We embrace, no longer Queen and adviser, but friends. A moment of pure love.

The gallas close in, surrounding us. 'Walk on, Inanna,' they say. 'We will take your adviser in your place.' I hold her in my arms and scream at them, 'I will never give her to you. Walk on!' They relent and we fly on to the great city of Umma, to the holy shrine. We spy my loyal servant, Shara, dressed in mourning clothes out of respect for my death. Once again, the gallas try to take him, and I refuse. We float on again, this time in search of another loyal servant. We find one, and upon seeing his funeral attire, I refuse once more. I will not allow my devoted servants to pay for my crime. I cannot. I will not.

And so, we return to my seat of my power, the great city of Uruk. It is then I know what to do. I know who needs to pay for their disloyalty, for their lack of respect. I see him by the big apple tree, seemingly joyful, without a care in the world. His royal garments shining in the bright sun, his body relaxed. He is playing his reed pipe, the pipe of the shepherds. This is not a man in mourning. Unlike my loyal servants who paid me proper funeral rites when I died in the underworld, this man is . . . well, blissful.

A familiar rage boils inside me, low at first in the pit of my stomach, then rising up and taking residence in my throat. I spit the following words in his direction: 'Take him! Take Dumuzi away! My husband!' The gallas swarm around him, as fear and horror flood his eyes.

His expression shifts and I notice something else, another emotion flickering. What is that dancing in his eyes? He stares into me, into my very soul: it is betrayal. Still, it has been commanded. They seize him, and begin to beat him, gashing him with axes. He cries out in pain. He raises his hands in supplication to Utu, god of justice. He appeals to Utu to transform his hands and feet into snakes so that the gallas can no longer hold him. Utu hears his cries and accepts his tears. Before our very eyes, Dumuzi is transformed. Hands and feet as slippery, slimy snakes, he breaks free and escapes his demons. As he disappears into the distance, the gallas muster behind him. It is only a matter of time. Death demands payment. But this time it will not be me.

I look out over the rooftops of Uruk, blood-red sunlight bouncing off the buildings, making the city resemble the burning embers of a hearth. A hearth that represents home, security, family and love. These are my people; they take me into their hearts, and I take them into mine. For I am more than just a girl, more than a mere goddess. I am Queen. I am Inanna.

Inanna's World

When thinking about this book, pondering its contents and asking myself which of these great ancient goddesses was going to make the cut, Inanna was an absolute dead cert. If we are looking for female deities that defy all modern notions of what it is to be 'feminine', ones that command us to look into the very core of ourselves with fresh eyes, Inanna is our girl. She is a goddess of so many 'contradictions': goddess of love, sexuality, war and the deification of the planet Venus. It is also interesting that she hails from one of the oldest pantheons of human civilisation, the Sumerian.

As we get acquainted with this goddess, transport yourself back in time, into her world. If you are feeling so inclined, you may even spend a few moments in quiet reverence to this goddess, channelling her energy and power to guide you in your own life. Ask yourself what messages are echoing through the ages, what is she whispering to you? After all, this is a book that invites you to find your own personal relationship with these mighty goddesses, to see what they still have to say to us today about our own femininity.

The tale of Inanna that you read at the start of this chapter was inspired by and based upon the amazing literary evidence that has survived from the Ancient Near East. These date back to approximately 2000 BCE as fragmentary clay tablets that are now scattered all over the world in various museums. This collection is vast in number, around five to six thousand, and brings to life the literary minds of the Sumerians and related cultures. Written in cuneiform, a writing system that uses distinct wedge-shaped characters, we can read epic tales, essays, fables and hymns, all of which describe in delicious detail this vibrant and spellbinding mythological tradition. Sumerologists – or academics that study the Sumerians – have pieced together the story of Inanna from these fragments. She is a goddess with a wealthy literary tradition, testament to her high status in Sumerian culture. In our myth above, we explore the Descent of Inanna, which is outlined in these tablets. Her sister, Ereshkigal, was worshipped as the queen of the underworld and guardian of the dead. I also used the famous Epic of Gilgamesh to provide extra context, namely gaps in the narrative that it could fill.

So, let's have a look at these people in greater detail. Sumerian culture is vast and complex; it would be remiss of me not to raise that here and temper your expectations. The origin of Sumerian culture is a matter of conjecture among academics even today. It is suspected to be one of the earliest known civilisations, dating from approx. 5500–1800 BCE. Furthermore, the picture is complicated by its ever-changing geographical boundaries, assimilating cultures, population fluctuations and social evolution. Loosely speaking, Sumer centres in the southerly aspects of the modern country of Iraq, bordered by the rivers Tigris and Euphrates. The people derived their name 'Sumerian' from the language they spoke. The picture is further con-fused by the overlapping civilisations that inhabited the area: Sumerian, Akkadian, Assyrian, Babylonian, Parthian and Mesopotamian to name a few. The latter of these, Mesopotamia, is most commonly used to denote the geographical region of southern-central Iraq and its sur-rounding areas. A sort of general label, given originally by the Ancient Greeks, to simplify the identity of the region. Some of the other labels are used to describe the dominating culture of the time and are therefore period specific. A very important point to note here is that some of these cultures shared deities. Our Inanna was conflated with an Akkadian goddess called Ishtar, something that will be discussed in finer detail later on. To cut to the chase, for us to build a coherent picture of the Sumerian goddess, it will be necessary to consider evidence from later periods and from associated cultures.

It is also important that we gain a little understanding of the difficulties we face regarding the evidence, as I allude to above. The scholarship on Sumerian culture is still in its relative infancy; in fact, it was not until the nineteenth century that the culture was even formally identified by archaeologists, seemingly engulfed by later cultures. It is here that we find our first warning sign – many have approached Sumerian culture through the lens of other cultures, which can make the evidence a tad difficult to unpick. The picture is blurred further by the fact that the evidence we have dating directly from the Sumerian period is scant, often archaeological, which is rarely found in original contexts. This is a problem, as how can academics draw accurate conclusions without numerous artefacts and/or defined contexts? Another consideration is that much of the literary and inscriptional evidence comes from the later Akkadian period, and although these cultures are entangled, this is problematic when attempting to hear a distinctly Sumerian voice. Finally, there is the matter of the conflagration of worship between the Sumerian deity Inanna and her Akkadian counterpart, Ishtar. In fact, so intertwined are these goddesses that academics can still not fully unravel them. There seems to be a general consensus that the worship of Inanna can be found at Uruk in the third and fourth millennia BCE, and therefore was in existence prior to the Akkadian Ishtar cult that flourished later on.

So how can we describe Sumerian culture? What might life have been like? The first question is easier to answer than the second. Sumer was a collection of city-states, roughly a dozen by the fourth millennium BCE. These were independently ruled, by a priestly governor (*ensi*) or a king (*lugal*), but it was the patron deity that took prime position. These cities were encircled by walls and contained houses within, made from bundled marsh reeds or mud bricks. The Sumerians were excellent irrigators, so you would also see channels of water bringing life to what would have been a relatively arid environment. This would have permitted agriculture, the lifeblood of these cities. However, by far the most dominating building will have been the *ziggurat*, a tiered, pyramidal temple dedicated to the preferred deity of that city.

For Inanna, the most prominent of these was her temple in the city of Uruk, one of the largest and most influential centres of Sumerian culture. Uruk was a thriving metropolis of trade, with six miles of defensive walls and a population of between forty thousand and eighty thousand people at its peak, a phenomenally large population for such an ancient culture. Some argue that, at one point, this city may have been the largest in the entire world. This sheer magnitude shows how important a deity Inanna must have been to have such a prominent role.

This is all well and good, but what did it feel like to live in these cities? What is known about the regular folk of Uruk is limited as much of the evidence is skewed towards the more elite members of society. Nonetheless, we can paint an exciting and vivid picture of daily life based largely on archaeological remains.

Imagine yourself transported back to Uruk, a bustling city, full of activity. The literal centre of your city is also likely the centre of your life – the ziggurat, imposing and dominating, as it watches over Uruk's inhabitants, Inanna's gaze upon you wherever you might be. Heading up to the courtyard of this complex, you might find market stalls, poets reciting verse, artists creating masterpieces, enslaved people running errands or a young boy racing through on his way to school (which were attached to temples). You may also visit the priests at the temple seeking advice or medical care, making offerings to appease the gods or spending a moment of solitude in your own private worship of the patron deity. Trade flourishes around you, goods flowing in and out of the city using the Euphrates and Tigris as trade routes. The wealthy are adorned with precious gems and metals sourced from far and wide. Perhaps you might be one of the many that left the city by day and tended to the neighbouring fields, cultivating your crop for sale at the next market. Underneath the shadow of the ziggurat would have been your home, a modest one for the poor, elaborate for the rich. Perhaps on a hot evening, you may even catch sight of someone sleeping on the flat roof to escape the stifling heat inside.

Despite the outward appearance of patriarchy, women had personal freedoms in the city. They could go freely to the marketplace, engage in trade, deal with their own legal issues, set up businesses and own property. Women from elite society could command great power in the role of head priestess, or even obtain official governmental positions.

However, life was not all sunshine and rainbows. Life expectancy was very low, around thirty-five for women and forty-five for men, according to extant skeletal remains. Women lived shorter lives due to the ongoing danger of childbirth. The threat of flooding, drought or starvation was a perpetual concern. For the vast majority, life would have been tough, with long days working in the fields, tending to animals and children and sourcing food. Slavery propped up society, and despite evidence of there being some social mobility for the lower classes, the harsh reality is that this would likely have been rare. It is easy to understand the role these powerful deities played in this treacherous game of life; why you might pin your every hope and desire and project every fear and worry onto them. It is easy to see how your patron goddess, Inanna, would be the buck at which everything stops. For these people, their lives were in her hands. Worshipping her, appeasing her, as she watched you from above, became the central aspect of a day in the life of a Sumerian.

But what of Inanna herself? What is her role in society? What does she represent? If you googled the name of this goddess, there would be one word that comes up unanimously: *complicated*. This is such a loaded term, fraught with modern connotations. Complicated to whom? To us today? To contemporary cultures? Inanna has associations with many areas, such as love, war, sexuality, beauty, political power and divine power. She is also associated with the planet Venus. This range is seemingly puzzling to the modern mind. How can one figure be associated closely with love and beauty, yet also be worshipped for her vengeance and violence? How can she be connected to fertility, yet never have her own children? To me, we are looking for answers in the wrong place. In order to unwrap Sumerian ideas of what it meant to be feminine, we must immediately and overtly acknowledge our own biases. To really hear Inanna, to tune into her voice, we must let go of modern notions of femininity and immerse ourselves in Sumerian culture, seeing her through the eyes of the people that worshipped her. This is no easy feat, as the evidence we have can be elusive. What I am proposing is radical: that perhaps she isn't really that complicated. That her so called 'contradictory nature' is actually *our* problem and not hers. Perhaps she has a great deal more to tell us today than we can realise – that femininity comes in all forms, even if some of those are not always embraced by modern communities. Wouldn't it be revolutionary to understand that the first civilisations embraced every type of feminine quality in their goddesses? Or further still, blurred the lines of masculine and feminine in her worship? That countless centuries and cultural influences have watered down and relegated femininity to a few acceptable aspects? That, just possibly, the first human civilisations knew exactly what femininity could include and worshipped it?

Gender, therefore, is at the heart of this discussion. There is a great deal of convincing evidence that suggests that the Sumerians had a fluid notion of gender identity. To begin with, there is conjecture regarding whether we can describe Sumerian languages as 'non gendered', where personal pronouns are not always used to denote a distinctly 'masculine' or 'feminine' gender but simply 'human' and 'non-human'. Some have argued that the Sumerians had a more open notion of gender and/or made allowances for a third type of gender. Inanna herself is often addressed as female in art and literature, yet she is also described in masculine terms. We can see this open notion of gender when we look at Inanna herself. We are told in multiple poetry fragments that Inanna had the ability to change a man into a woman and vice versa. However, there is still a great deal of debate among linguists as to the exact understanding of Sumerian languages, so this is something we need to consider when attempting to understand their self-expression.

It is well documented that Inanna's cultic attendants were described as gender fluid. At her festivals, men dressed as women and women dressed as men; some of her priests practised same sex behaviours and there is evidence of eunuchs (castrated males) in her temple. But perhaps the most fascinating group of worshippers were the *gala* priests. They have their origins in poetic myth and were described as a type of people created by the god Enki to sing to Inanna and soothe her incandescent rage. They sung in a dialect, often used by female characters, that was called *eme-sal*. Some *gala* also adopted female names, or became wives. What does this all mean for our examination of feminine qualities? In my view, the evidence for gender fluidity points to Inanna's powers to assign gender. It is her divine mandate to create others in her own image, to embrace all aspects of our human qualities through the so-called disruption of gender normative behaviour. So, are these priests adopting this behaviour because the cult of Inanna provided a safe context for one to express their gender freely, or is this about a reflective devotion to a goddess who transcends boundaries? Maybe it is both. Either way, this is one facet of her character worth considering.

Inanna's connection to sexuality does not stop there. There is one famous (and often eyebrow raising) quote from Inanna in the story of her courtship to her future husband Dumuzi, in which she asks: 'Who will plough my vulva?' If you have a sensitive temperament, this may shock, although it must be noted that Sumerian culture probably had a more open notion of sexuality – as I am sure is becoming apparent the more you read! Inanna's relationship to sexual behaviour is complex and vast. In addition to the same sex love described above, there is evidence that she was associated with marital sex, prostitution and adultery. It has often been noted that it is unusual for a goddess to be married, but never have her own children. To not have dominion over domestic situations, childbirth or other female related domains. This is why I have chosen Inanna; she is curious, different. Another aspect of this connected Inanna to the royal authority of the serving king through a rite known as the 'sacred marriage'. In this union, a king would seek legitimacy for his rule by having sexual union with Inanna in her temple after making offerings outside. Through the act of sacred marriage, whereby Inanna would symbolically marry and have sex with either the high priest or the king of the land (through a human conduit), she would adorn her husband/lover with her political powers and martial prowess. It was thought that this marriage would grant the king a successful rule, both in battle and otherwise. We see here another aspect of Inanna's power, bestowment of divine power in male rule. Therefore, in a Sumerian context, even one with male rulers, feminine divine power is sought. It is the intertwining of the masculine and feminine that creates this power, upholds it and nourishes it.

Inanna's darker side is also important. Her association with war and revenge was strong, as we can see in the retelling above. In fact, in many of the hymns to Inanna, this vengeful and ferocious nature was perhaps one of the more highlighted elements of her various qualities. Inanna was often invoked as the protectoress of the kings of the land. In fact, Sargon of Akkad, the first great ruler of the Akkadian Empire, claimed her support in battle and politics. In this way it seemed war and power were intertwined. As such, it makes sense that as her literal power was intertwined with whatever ruling force there was at the time, any aspect of political power or war could be connected to her. You can imagine how fearful of her this would make the people of Sumer. For this reason, they appeased her through various rituals, worship and hymn – always afraid that they might displease her, and her wrath might be unleashed upon this earth, like we see in the story above.

Her association with the planet Venus is intriguing. This planet, often visible to the naked eye, was seen as the 'morning star' in many ancient cultures. Also called the eight-pointed star, it was one of the most prolific symbols associated with Inanna, found on boundary stones and cylindrical seals. It may have been that the enslaved people that worked in Ishtar's temple were branded with this star. Interestingly, it has been suggested that the story of the descent of Inanna was a way for Sumerians to explain the cycle of Venus's movement. Inanna could represent Venus, and her movement in and out of the underworld replicates the motion of Venus (in relation to other planets) in the night sky. In this way, Inanna is made eternal, as she watches over her worshippers. It is also very interesting to trace the story of Inanna in Sumer, through Ishtar in Akkadian culture, through Astarte in the Canaanite tradition (the region that includes areas of Israel, Lebanon, Jordan and Syria) and possibly through to Aphrodite in Greece, who then becomes, yes you guessed it, Venus in Roman mythology.

Seemingly, the thin line between life and death, prosperity and damnation, harmony and chaos were the remit of this goddess. This is not to say that some of these are specific only to Inanna; in fact, it could be argued that these are the traits of many a divine figure. But what makes her unique and fascinating is that she is capable of such violence *and* could encourage great love. She sits on the thrones of both creation and destruction. How can one figure be an icon both for love and sex as well as for war and rage? Well, I would argue easily! Let's have a real look at the nature of women, or even at all of humanity. We are made to be multifaceted creatures, capable of a vast range of emotions and therefore actions. However, over time, men and women have been typecast and moulded into distinct images. Men are supposed to be strong, powerful, angry and consistent, and women are soft, sensitive, caring and kind. But Inanna blurs all of these gender norms, which I might add are a load of baloney. Isn't it so powerful to think back to one of the earliest cultures we know of, and see that their concept of femininity included the so-called masculine? That she was revered for her power, her violence? In

Sumerian culture, divine expression of the female allowed for her to be all things. She is, in fact, not full of contradictions, opposites and polarities. Instead, she asks us to drop our labels and truly consider human traits in their totality. Femininity, in her eyes, is a movable object. Swaying and dancing with the breeze of life, one thing in one moment, another the next. Changeable, adaptable and, let's be honest, a much more realistic picture of what is means to be feminine today.

Gender identity aside, we all possess a spectrum of these qualities, and they shapeshift, depending on the day, the week, the year. Inanna asks us to look at ourselves, in totality, and accept the many facets of what it means to be a female, without judgement. How freeing it is to embrace her energy and accept all parts of ourselves fully. So, the next time you are judged for being too inconsistent, too masculine, too feminine – remember Inanna. For there once was an icon that would help you embrace all aspects of self. Don't you think it's time we reclaimed her for ourselves?

KALI

Hindu Goddess of Time, Death and Destruction

Kali

Hindu Goddess of Time,
Death and Destruction

The Dark Mother

And so, I was born. Into this this world, with a specific purpose. To kill. To strike fear into the hearts of demons, the ones that oppose the great gods themselves. As such, I have been made to look this way. I look down at my arms, for I have many. In one of my left hands, I hold my *khadga*, my curved sword, ready to attack. It is seen to be the embodiment of divine wisdom. In my other left hand, I hold a severed head, a symbol of the human ego. I keep it next to divine wisdom so that it may be perpetually overpowered by it – allowing for enlightenment. I hold specific poses, *mudras*, with my left arms, one showing my fearlessness and one my blessing. It reminds my devotees to worship me well to receive the gifts I can bestow, the guidance I can give. I also carry a trident, my *trishula*, and a *kapala*, a skull cup in which I collect all of the blood that pours from the severed head. And then there is my garland, the *mundamala*, either 108 human heads or fifty-one, the former symbolising the beads of a mala, the latter the garland letters of the beautiful ancient language of my people, Sanskrit. The holy and ancient land of India is my home, but as my people travel, so do I. India: the land of shimmering suns, of great rivers, like the Ganges, that provides life to all. A land of colour: bright pinks, reds, yellows, blues and greens, as vibrant as the people of this wonderful place. A contrast against the darkness of my own skin.

Sometimes people change my appearance, and so I slip and shift, like the sands of time, to be this thing or another, something to one person, another to someone else. Perhaps I have more arms, or my black skin is turned a deep, dark blue. My name, Kali, comes from the Sanskrit word for black, for this colour absorbs all others. Sometimes my mouth is red, dripping with the blood of those I have devoured, tongue protruding, eyes and hair wild. And so it has been, I morph, adapt and change in the eyes of those that worship me, becoming their Kali, their goddess. But always fearsome, always dark, always bloodthirsty.

To really understand me, beyond these images, is to know me, know my story. See behind that veil of darkness, peer into my blackness, hold the gaze of my bloody red eyes to see me, the true me. Nothing is as it seems in this world; and this I believe people learn the hardest of ways, through their trials, pain and fears. For I am ancient, as old as time itself, and I have truths inside me for those who wish to see. Do not misunderstand me, miscategorise me. Simply sit and listen, for I will tell you who I really am.

Many, many years ago, at a time when gods and demons roamed this earth, I was born. I came into this world at the intersection of light and dark, from the rage of the great goddess Durga. It is she who cradles us all, with both the gentleness and the fierce protectiveness of a mother, the one who will speak soothing words in one moment and kill anything threatening in the next, with no remorse. It is from this quality that I am made. Although I embody the rage of the great mother, the fire that fuels it is a great love. The kind of burning, passionate and powerful love that only a mother can know. A protective quality that can destroy anything in its path. Something that is ignited in every mother who holds her baby in her arms for the first time, for every animal that licks her cub. It is a primal, natural and a powerful force like no other. It is nurture personified, and this nurture has a dark side. The side where there is no cost too high to protect your creation. Go here and you will find me.

I remember the first time I opened my eyes, to see the face of Mother Durga. I looked down at my arms, and before I noticed how many I had, I fixated on their colour. I understood immediately that she and I are as one, that she created me for a purpose. Even now, I can feel the pulse of that purpose beating in my veins, as strongly as the day

I came to this earth. It is *Shakti*, a divine and cosmic feminine force, governing all of creation. Without this energy, nothing would exist. It was this force that bade me open my eyes that first time, gaze up at Durga and see the Shakti glowing inside us. Without words, I knew what I was being asked to do. *Protect*. At any cost.

I looked around me and noticed carnage. Demons, or *Rakshasas*, running lose over the beauty of creation, threatening to destroy it all. Their monstrous appearance was equally terrifying, with protruding fangs and long, sharp claws. They can shapeshift, making them even more difficult to identify and adding to their horror. But there is no force greater than me, than the embodiment of protective rage – and so I struck, and I struck hard, with no mercy. Firstly, I fixed my gaze on the demons harassing Mother Durga herself. I slayed the demons, Chanda and Munda, with cool ease. Their heads lolled in the dust, mouths agape in horror of their demise. Barely a moment to comprehend what had just befallen them. But these demons were small, insignificant against the mightiness of the demon Raktabīja. Many gods had tried and failed to stop him, for he has a terrorising power like none other. Every time he spilled a drop of blood in battle, another demon of equal strength and size sprang up from the ground. He represents the worst kind of threat, a perpetual one, a type that attacks all of creation again and again. He needed to be stopped.

My eyes began to bulge, my arms raised high, sword still

dripping with the blood of Chanda and Munda. My long red tongue darted out, all parts of me poised for battle. The Shakti inside of me swelled and rose to my call, flowing rapidly through my body, with the force of a thousand rivers overflowing their banks, running wild and untamed across the landscape. Like this, my Shakti drove me forward, toes grazing the dust in the ground as I glided through the many clones of Raktabīja. Each time I swung my sword and drove it deep into the flesh of a demon, I would use my long tongue to lap up any blood so none was spilled, and no more demons could be created. As I swallowed, my Shakti surrounded the blood inside me, squeezing the darkness out of it until it was transformed into light, transmuted into something whole. And so, with each gulp, balance was restored. Transmutation was occurring. Mother. Protector. Creator. Destroyer.

Before long, all the cloned demons were vanquished, and I came face to face with Raktabīja himself. I looked up at him, huge creature that he was. Skin the colour of bright red blood, long black horns protruding from his forehead, fangs hanging down from his huge mouth. He seemed to smile at me, the arrogance of a demon who believed he could not be slain. But I could see through the smile, into the demon's deeper self. And that part of him was afraid. Very afraid. I raised a blood-curdling scream, flew up into the sky, arms wide, sword above my head, soaring higher and higher until the blue hue of earth gradually turned to black, and I was floating in the stars. I hovered, a moment of calm before the madness, then dived headfirst back down into the earth, so fast, and sliced through Raktabīja's neck with such force that the blood began to spurt upwards in a column. Before his head even reached the ground, I drank the blood quickly so he could be fully overpowered by the Shakti inside me. Not until I consumed the last drop, did I fall to my knees and let out a scream. I screamed the scream of a mother's vengeance. The rage and fury left me, sweet balance soothed my aching body.

And so it is. I live between worlds. I exist in the margins between life and death. I have come to be worshipped as a goddess of all time, as a manifestation of the ebb and flow of life through space. For what can create and destroy as capably as time? With one of my many hands I give, I create. With one of the others, I take, I destroy. Everything in this world is time-bound. You borrow energy and you return it. There is no end, only transformation.

Look carefully at me; really see me. My truth lies in the subtleties. Peer deeply. You will see that beyond my wild, mad and violent appearance is the gesture for reassurance and safety, the *abhayamudrā*. Take me into your heart and I will offer this protection to you. Always.

Kali's world

The story above has been adapted and imagined, but is based upon the *Devi Mahatmyam*, a Hindu philosophical text from around 550 BCE. It explores the goddess as she is represented in her many forms, as the ultimate power in the universe – awesome, isn't it? The seven hundred verses that make up this manuscript describe a storied battle between bad and good forces. It's a phenomenal piece of work, which on its own provides a fascinating take on the world of feminine divine power, the workings of the universe and much more. I find it utterly wonderful that we have an ancient script that tells us about the very essence of ourselves that we seem to have forgotten. I highly recommend reading it and reminding yourself of your true feminine power.

As Kali is a goddess of the Hindu religion, we must begin here to understand her more fully. We have already met Hinduism in our chapter on Rangda, but in this chapter we will focus on Hinduism in India. Hinduism is one of the world's oldest religions, with a history dating back over four millennia. It finds its roots in the Indian subcontinent and has evolved through countless ages, cultures and philosophies. Tracing the exact origins of this religion is very difficult, with a variety of conflicting dates given. It is likely that the earliest Hindu practices date to around 3000 BCE, with the religion changing and adapting as various cultural and historical elements leave their mark. The countless infusions of ideas and beliefs played a significant role in shaping what we now recognise as Hinduism. As a person of mixed-race heritage from this region, through Pakistan, I find this deeply problematic and painful. There is a great deal to say about the negative impact of British colonialism in South Asia, but it is sadly beyond the scope of this book.

Needless to say, the repercussions of British rule in India have left an indelible mark on this beautiful country.

As a result of various influences, the religious landscape of ancient India was a diverse tapestry of beliefs and practices, with no central religious authority, making it challenging to pinpoint a single origin. Hinduism's pantheon is vast, comprising countless deities, each with distinct attributes and stories. At its core, Hinduism is a polytheistic faith (a faith with many gods), but it also acknowledges a supreme reality, often referred to as *Brahman*, which is formless and transcendent. Key figures in Hinduism include Brahma, the creator; Vishnu, the preserver; and Shiva, the destroyer and transformer. These deities are often worshipped in various forms and avatars, depending on specific traditions and beliefs. The goddess Devi, in her many forms like Durga, Kali and Saraswati, plays an essential role in Hinduism, symbolising the feminine divine and the creative, nurturing aspect of existence called Shakti.

One of the foundational texts of Hinduism is the *Vedas*, a collection of ancient scriptures that form the basis of religious knowledge and rituals. These texts, written in Sanskrit, contain hymns, chants and philosophical discussions that provide insight into the early spiritual practices of ancient India. The Vedic Period, roughly between 1500 and 500 BCE, is a crucial phase in the development of Hinduism. The Vedas introduced key concepts that continue to shape Hinduism, among them *Karma* (the moral law of cause and effect), *Dharma* (duty or righteousness) and reincarnation (the belief in the cycle of birth, death and rebirth). Around 600 BCE, the *Upanishads,* a collection of philosophical texts, emerged. They laid the groundwork for several schools of philosophical thought within Hinduism, including *Vedanta* and *Samkhya.* The epic narratives of the *Mahabharata* and the *Ramayana* are also significant in Hinduism, containing devotional and philosophical material essential to Hindu thinking. In the sixth century BCE, the historical figure Siddhartha Gautama, known as the Buddha, founded Buddhism, a religion that emerged from the religious and philosophical landscape of India. Buddhism and Hinduism coexisted and influenced each other for centuries, with some Buddhist ideas making their way into Hindu philosophy. The spread of Hinduism beyond India's borders, particularly to South East Asia, was facilitated through trade and cultural exchanges. Hindu temples, sculptures and art became prevalent in various regions, reflecting the adaptability and inclusiveness of the religion. It is clear that the history of the Hindu religion is a vast and intricate journey that spans millennia. It has evolved and adapted to changing times while maintaining its core principles and practices. Today, Hinduism remains a vibrant and dynamic faith, embraced by millions worldwide, and continues to evolve in this ever-changing, fast-paced world.

What might it look like to practise this religion? In Hinduism, the rituals and ceremonies are diverse, ranging from daily prayers and offerings at home shrines to those in grand temple festivals. Pilgrimage to sacred sites like

Varanasi in Uttar Pradesh in north India, the Ganges River that flows across India and Bangladesh, and the temples of Tamil Nadu in southern India are one of many religious experiences for Hindus. Some Hindu temples are stunning places, utterly ornate and gilded with precious materials like gold, marble and granite, often carved with spellbinding detail. These are places of divinity, with opulence and beauty that make you feel complete awe. Yoga and meditation, integral components of Hinduism, are pathways to spiritual growth and self-realisation. The practice of meditation – seeking to connect with the divine within – is at the heart of many Hindu traditions. These practices are now widespread throughout the world, and incredibly popular in the West. Throughout its long history, Hinduism has absorbed and integrated numerous cultural and religious influences, resulting in a diverse and multifaceted faith. It's a religion that has shown remarkable resilience and adaptability, capable of accommodating a myriad of beliefs and practices. In essence, Hinduism defies easy categorisation or summary. Its beauty lies in its complexity, its ability to encompass a multitude of beliefs and practices, and a rich tapestry of mythology, philosophy, rituals and spirituality. It continues to be a source of inspiration and enlightenment worldwide, providing profound insight into the human experience and our eternal quest for meaning.

Hindu worship, also known as *Puja*, is a beautiful practice that is deeply personal to each individual. Imagine it like this: you have a favourite deity or maybe even a couple, like picking your favourite characters in a story. It's your way of connecting with the divine, and it can vary quite a bit from one person to another. First, you'd set up a special place for your worship, usually at home. This could be a small altar or a dedicated corner where you place images or idols of your chosen deities. You want to make it feel sacred. Now, to get in the right mindset, you might start with meditation. It's like a mental warm-up, calming your thoughts and focusing your mind on the divine. After that, you might recite some prayers, mantras or hymns, dedicated to your chosen deity – kind of like having a heart-to-heart with the god. Light plays a big role in Hindu worship. You'd light incense sticks and oil lamps, which represent dispelling darkness and spreading divine light. Think of it as a way to brighten your spiritual connection. Flowers are another important offering. Marigolds are especially popular, and you'd arrange them nicely on the altar. Now, the food part is interesting. You offer food to your deity, which is believed to become blessed once offered. This food, called *Prasada* is then shared among the worshippers as a way to spread blessings. Holy water also comes into play. It's often water from sacred rivers like the Ganges. Sprinkling a little on yourself and your offerings is like a spiritual refreshment. Hinduism loves symbols and sacred geometry, so you might use things like *Yantras* (geometric diagrams) during meditation. They help you focus your thoughts, like a visual aid in your connection. Sometimes, Hindus fast on specific days dedicated to their deity. It's seen as a way to cleanse the body and mind – a detox for your soul. You visit the temple, offer your prayers, and maybe even participate in organised rituals led by priests. Festivals are a huge deal. Envisage them like the ultimate fan conventions. They're dedicated to different deities, and they involve elaborate rituals, parades and group worship. It's a big celebration. There are many different festivals, but perhaps one of the most well known is Holi. Taking place in spring, it celebrates the deities Krishna and Radha and signifies the triumph of good over evil. People gather near bonfires and sing and dance; they also spray coloured water, which is perhaps the most recognisable aspect of the celebration. It's a beautiful festival, filled with love and laughter. Outside of these big public celebrations, the most crucial thing to remember is that Hindu worship is intensely personal. It's not just rituals; it's about love, devotion and seeking a deeper connection with the divine. It is your personal connection, or how sacredness dwells within you, that is most important.

Hinduism has moulded Indian culture in more ways than one. Its very essence is woven into the societal structures and cultural practices of this fascinating country. From ancient to modern, it endures and continues to shape its people. For instance, the concept of dharma guides people in fulfilling their obligations in family, society and their chosen profession. The philosophical concepts of Hinduism, such as Vedanta and yoga, have played a pivotal role in Indian philosophical thought and continue to be studied and practised today. Because Hinduism places a strong emphasis on values like truth, non-violence, compassion and self-discipline, these values have left a profound mark on Indian ethics and morality.

The religion has also impacted Indian societal structures. In India, social hierarchy is based on something called the *caste* system. This system categorises individuals in different groups based on their occupation and birth, and is underpinned by patriarchal ideas. Despite official condemnation of caste-based discrimination in modern India, its influence can still be observed in various aspects of society, including marriage and social interactions. In the intricate tapestry of India's caste system, the role of women unfolds with layers of complexity, shaped by tradition and changing societal norms. Within this framework, women have faced varying degrees of privilege and oppression.

Traditionally, the caste system divided Indian society into four major *Varnas*, or classes: *Brahmins* (priests and scholars), *Kshatriyas* (warriors and rulers), *Vaishyas* (merchants and farmers) and *Shudras* (labourers and service providers). Beyond these Varnas, there existed a fifth group – those considered 'untouchables', or *Dalits*, who were often relegated to the most marginalised and degrading roles in society. There is much to say about the impact of a system like this on a society but as you can imagine it would take an entire book to do this justice. So, setting these debates aside, it is important to focus our attention on the experience of life for women in these different groups. That is not to say men do not worship Kali, but as we are interested in the personal relationship she has with women, we will concentrate there.

Both past and present, women's roles are intricately tied to their caste identity, with each caste imposing distinct expectations and restrictions. In Brahmin families, women are often expected to embody the ideals of purity and devotion, primarily fulfilling domestic roles as mothers and homemakers. While education was traditionally reserved for Brahmin boys, some Brahmin girls received instruction in religious texts. Yet, they rarely hold positions of authority within religious institutions. Kshatriya women enjoy a somewhat elevated status compared to many other castes, as they often played important roles in maintaining family honour and lineage. Some take on political responsibilities when their husbands were away, wielding influence in governance. However, their agency is still curtailed by societal norms. Vaishya women contribute to the family's economic endeavours, participating in trade and agriculture. They have a more active presence in public life compared to Brahmin women, often managing businesses alongside their husbands. Nevertheless, the overarching patriarchal structure limits their independence. Shudra women, as part of the labourer and service-provider caste, face numerous challenges. They often work as agricultural labourers or domestic servants, enduring strenuous labour. Educational opportunities are scarce, and they have limited mobility and social status. For Dalit women, the caste system imposes harsher forms of discrimination. Dalit women face not only gender-based discrimination but also the dehumanising effects of untouchability, which persisted for generations and remains a live issue in India today. Statistically speaking, around one in ten Dalit women are victims of sexual assault each day, and with Dalit women making up around eighty million members of the population, those are huge numbers. There is a very long way to go before these women achieve the social justice they so deserve.

It also must be noted that there exists an issue of colourism within this caste system. In case you are new to the term, colourism is the prejudice or discrimination within an ethnic group favouring those with lighter skin tones. It has its origins within the caste system: as lower socio-economic classes worked outside, they tended to have darker skin, and so fairer skinned people became synonymous with the upper classes and intelligence. So entrenched is the issue, that skin bleaching has become a very popular treatment, in fact representing around 50 per cent of the skincare market in India. I do not need to point out the problem with this, and the personal cost for people of darker skin tones.

Over time, India has undergone significant social changes, and women's roles within the caste system have evolved. Education and economic opportunities have expanded for women across castes. Legal reforms have aimed to address gender discrimination, such as laws against domestic violence. However, it's essential to acknowledge that the caste system still persists in various forms, perpetuating inequalities and hierarchies. Women continue to grapple with intersecting challenges related to gender, caste and class. Progress has been made, but the journey towards gender equity and social justice in India remains a complex and ongoing struggle, shaped by the intricate interplay of caste and gender dynamics. It is not hard to see how the worship of divine feminine goddesses, like Kali, could have a profoundly inspiring effect on women within this system.

Hopefully you now have a clearer picture of the religion and society that our goddess belongs to. But what of her? What roles does she play in all of this? Kali is part of a formidable group of female deities, all of whom possess Shakti – divine feminine energy. They embody various feminine qualities, reflecting the multifaceted nature of the feminine divine.

Let's explore a few prominent Hindu goddesses before we head on over to Kali. Durga is often depicted as a fierce and powerful warrior goddess who rides a lion and wields multiple weapons. She is revered as a protector of the universe, particularly against evil forces and negativity. Durga's story is often associated with her victory over the demon Mahishasura, symbolising the triumph of good over evil. She is the one that births Kali from her forehead in our retelling. There is also Lakshmi, the goddess of wealth, prosperity and fortune. She is often depicted with lotus flowers and is believed to bring material and spiritual abundance to her devotees. Lakshmi is worshipped during Diwali, the festival of lights, to invite her blessings for a prosperous year ahead. Saraswati is the goddess of knowledge, wisdom and the arts. She is often portrayed playing a musical instrument and holding a book. Students and scholars often invoke her blessings for success in their academic pursuits. Parvati is the goddess of love, devotion and fertility, understood to be a loving wife and mother to her two sons, Ganesha and Kartikeya. Parvati symbolises the ideal of feminine strength and grace. Together, these goddesses represent divine feminine energy and are an essential component to cosmic power. We need to understand this context to grasp the wider power that Kali possesses.

Kali is one of the most formidable goddesses of Hinduism, and she holds a profound and complex importance deeply woven into the cultural and religious tapestry of India. Her worship and symbolism extend beyond religion, leaving an indelible mark on art, literature and philosophy. Kali's name, derived from the Sanskrit word *Kāla*, meaning time, serves as a reminder of the impermanence of all things. She symbolises the cyclical nature of creation, preservation and destruction, emphasising the ever-changing course of existence. In her role as a triumphant force, Kali often vanquishes evil demons, symbolising the victory of good over evil and the ultimate triumph of truth and righteousness. The symbolism of Kali's form carries profound spiritual meanings. Her destructive power signifies the dissolution of the material world, including attachments, desires and the ego. This annihilation process is viewed as a transformative path towards spiritual awakening.

Goddess Kali is worshipped annually at the *Kali Puja*, a Hindu festival celebrated primarily in the Indian states of West Bengal, Assam and parts of Odisha as well as the country of Bangladesh. This typically occurs during the new moon night of the Hindu lunar month of *Ashwin*, which usually falls in October or November in the Gregorian calendar. Kali Puja holds immense significance for devotees who seek the blessings of Goddess Kali for protection from evil forces, spiritual empowerment and liberation from ignorance and suffering. While Kali is often perceived as a fearsome deity, her devotees believe that she destroys negative energies and impurities to pave the way for new beginnings. In West Bengal, Kali Puja is one of the most important festivals, showcasing the rich cultural heritage of Bengal and the deep reverence for Goddess Kali. In Kolkata, the capital of West Bengal, *Kali Puja pandals* (marquees) are often adorned with intricate decorations, stunning materials covering the inside, with a statue of Kali dressed in fine robes, flower garlands and precious jewellery. It attracts large crowds of visitors and devotees from all walks of life. Worshippers often come at night, under the new moon, with offers of red hibiscus flowers, sweets, rice and lentils to honour the goddess. In terms of more personal ritualistic worship, people honour Kali in their homes with clay sculptures and offerings. Kali Puja is a spiritually charged festival that celebrates the divine energy of Goddess Kali. It reflects the duality of life, acknowledging both creation and destruction as essential aspects of existence. While deeply rooted in religious traditions, Kali Puja is also a time for cultural celebrations and community gatherings, bringing people together to seek the blessings of the fearsome yet benevolent goddess.

However, Kali's significance is not limited to religious circles. She has influenced art, literature and popular culture. Her image can be found in contemporary Indian literature and cinema, often used to challenge societal norms and provoke thought. Kali's symbolism in art represents rebellion, change and the breaking of boundaries. Moreover, Kali's influence extends to social and political movements. Her image is sometimes invoked in protests and rallies, signifying the power of the people to bring about change. She is regarded as a symbol of resistance against oppression, injustice and discrimination. In the broader context of Indian spirituality, Kali highlights the cyclical nature of time; that creation and destruction are essential components of existence. Her worship aligns with the belief in the impermanence of life and the need to confront and overcome challenges and obstacles. It's important to note that Kali's significance varies among individuals and communities. While some see her as a deity to be venerated and worshipped traditionally, others view her as a symbol of rebellion and empowerment. These diverse interpretations outline Kali's adaptability and the multifaceted nature of her significance in modern India.

Kali also teaches modern women the importance of self-empowerment. In a global context where women still face discrimination, violence and inequality, Kali's unapologetic strength serves as a icon of resilience. Modern women can draw inspiration to stand up for their rights, pursue their ambitions and break free from societal constraints. One of the most significant lessons Kali imparts is the power of self-expression. She is often depicted as a wild and untamed force of nature, unafraid to be herself. In a world that often tries to confine women to narrow roles and expectations, Kali encourages authenticity. Her image as a destroyer of evil forces signifies the strength needed to challenge and dismantle oppressive systems, inspiring modern women when facing the obstacles and injustices they encounter. Furthermore, Kali's story emphasises the importance of balance. She is both a fierce warrior and a loving mother. In modern society, women often juggle various responsibilities, and Kali's example encourages them to find harmony and embrace all aspects of their identity. Goddess Kali also embodies the power of female solidarity. Her story often involves alliances with other goddesses, highlighting the strength that comes from women supporting each other.

However, what perhaps stands out most for me – and is the inspiration behind my retelling in this chapter – is that Kali teaches us to look beyond appearances. All of her inner wisdom can be easily swallowed up in the narrative of her darker side. Of her outwardly terrifying image. That looks can be deceiving. That truth lies within. To anyone not familiar with Kali's rich and multifaceted symbolism, she can simply look like, well, a terrifying deity. But she is much more than that, and each aspect of her physical appearance has a tale to tell. Kali is often depicted with a jet-black or dark blue complexion. This dark skin symbolises her all-encompassing nature, as the colour black is associated with the infinite and the mysterious. Sometimes, Kali is depicted with blue skin, particularly in South India. This blue complexion is connected to the infinite sky and cosmic space. It also represents the eternal darkness that existed before the creation of the universe.

Kali is typically portrayed with four, eight, ten or even eighteen arms. Each arm holds various weapons and symbols, emphasising her immense power, her ability to protect her devotees, as well as a visual representation of her multitasking divine nature. Kali's face bears a fierce and intense expression, with her tongue protruding. Her tongue is often seen as a symbol of her wrath and thirst for the blood of demons and evil forces. It also signifies the act of destroying evil by consuming it. She is adorned with a garland or necklace made of severed heads. Each of these heads represents one of the ego's tenets, symbolising her triumph over human ego and ignorance. It serves as a reminder of the impermanence of life and the futility of material attachments. Kali is often depicted wearing a skirt made of severed human arms, which highlight her role as the ultimate destructor of ego and attachment – the liberation of the soul from worldly bonds. Her nurturing and protective nature contrasts with her fearsome appearance, emphasising her dual role as both a loving mother and a

fierce protector. In some cases, Kali stands with one foot on
the chest of her consort, Lord Shiva. This characterises her
dominance over time and the material world. Lord Shiva,
in this context, represents passive, unmanifested time,
while Kali is active, manifest time. Kali's primary weapons
are a sword and a trident. The sword is divine knowledge,
which has the power to cut through ignorance and delu-
sion, and the trident has the power to destroy evil forces
and maintain cosmic order. Imitations of Kali are often in
a dancing posture, known as the 'Dance of Destruction' or
the 'Dance of Death' – a cycle of creation, preservation and
destruction in the universe.

What does all of this demonstrate to us? That each aspect
of Kali's physical appearance has something else to tell us.
Beyond the detailed and rich symbolism of her Hindu faith,
Kali asks us to look past what you first see. That deep and
wondrous truths lie behind the mask. That we ought to
discover the feminine motivations within us – the character, personality, drive, ambition – and even the soul. That
if something appears scary, unfriendly and, let's be real,
terrifying, it is often growing out of something good. Look
deeply. Judge not. Our femininity is layered. And sometimes those layers have a fearsome outer shell. Kali asks us
to embrace it all, in ourselves, and in others.

MAWU-LISA

Vodun Goddess of All Creation, the Sun and the Moon

Mawu-Lisa

*Vodun Goddess of All Creation,
the Sun and the Moon*

The Breath

We sit. We look. We feel. The breeze gently kisses our cheeks, cooling them as it brushes past. The fierce, hot sun burns into our forehead, and a bead of sweat slowly travels down the side of our face, finding its final resting place on the lush green canopy below. We float. We glide. We soar. We examine all that we have created. Vast swathes of green trees, in all shades – from deep olives to a green that is so dark it almost appears black. We marvel at how they blend and mesh together. We swoop down into them, ducking through the canopy and feeling the humidity of the atmosphere hit us. We place our feet on the ground and begin to walk, leaves crushed beneath our feet. We scan the jungle and use all of our senses to drink in our creation.

We close our eyes. We hear the loud calling of the monkey, the growl of the jungle cat and the squawking of the parrot. When our eyes flutter open, we see colours. All of the colours, bright white and red flowers; orange and yellow fruits and the blue sky peaking in through the trees. Eyes closed again, we breath deeply as the fragrance of life hits our nostrils. We sit, back firm against the mighty teak tree. We stretch our long dark limbs in front of us and notice how our skin glistens in the heat of the late-afternoon sun. Time passes. The light changes, first bright, almost blinding, then milky, pale – weaker. Night has come. The stars and the moon twinkle in the sky like precious jewels. We feel the beautiful, life-giving air. Both of us, twins. Mawu, the feminine, Lisa the masculine, bound together in one body, in perfect harmony. We smile. So, there it is, the first day of Life on Earth.

Then, we feel it. The worry. The weight of all creation. Both physical and emotional. We realise that something must be done to protect and strengthen this beauty, this wondrousness that is all Life. We begin to fear that the world is too heavy, unsupported and vulnerable to collapse. For this Earth is floating on water, as water is the source of all Life. The rain, springs, lakes and seas nourish the Earth and allow plants to grow, animals to drink. But perhaps it could sink; perhaps the sky might collapse in on itself and destroy it all . . .

We think, and we think hard. How can we solve this problem? Then we have it. We call upon the great serpent,

Aido Hwedo, to visit us. She comes, her slippery, scaly, slimy belly dragging along this lush ground. As she zigzags towards us, we marvel at how she moves – no, glides – fluidly along the ground. As if she is married to it, as if her body and the soil are one. For she has been our companion in the birthing of this world – we rode inside her mouth as we breathed Life into it, and she in turn gave the land its curves. She carved canyons, valleys, mountains and rivers. She is as much of it as we are.

She approaches, and we speak. 'Aido Hwedo, we need your help. This great Earth we have created needs support. We fear it may collapse if we do not work together to strengthen it. We ask if you will coil up and hold together both the Earth and the Heavens, so that they do not fold in on themselves. Is this something you can do?'

The serpent looks up at us, and full of love and care, she nods in agreement. And so it came to be that the Earth was held up by a great serpent. When she is unhappy, or restless, the Earth shakes as she moves her gargantuan body beneath its surface. When she coils and moves in a circle, the Earth spins. If she is not fed by the Earth's minerals, she will eat herself, and one day the world will cease to be without the support of her great back. As life is given, it is taken away. This is the way of things. With the land held up by Aido Hwedo, we sigh, a deep release, and a strong wind travels across the lands.

A new day arrives. We awaken to a dazzling blue sky, sun strong and fiercely hot as it rises. Lisa loves the sun, for he created it and it carries his energy. Within its intense heat lie the masculine energies – strength, toughness, war, work and power. Mawu, however, prefers the moon, with its feminine qualities of rest, joy, nurture, calm, gentleness and fertility. Together we dance in perpetuity, a cosmic dance, a blissful unison of our nature. Neither one nor the other superior, but instead both equal. In balance. In endless synchronicity.

Energies aligned; we begin our day's work. We want to populate this great Earth with more creation. We call upon our great servant, Awe, the monkey, to assist in making more animals out of clay, into which we can breathe Life, or *Sekpoli*. Only we have this power, it is the beauty that unfolds from our harmony, the mingling together of the masculine and the feminine to create Life. And so, it is. Awe comes, he nods in understanding and climbs back down the palm tree to get on with the important work of making Life.

But a monkey is a tricky creature, we made him so. Instead of doing our bidding, he rushes to the other animals and begins to boast about his ability to breathe Life. We hear him chattering away, first to the zebra on the plains, then to the crocodile in the swamp. We watch. We watch as he travels from place to place, falsely claiming this power. That is until he reaches the village. Here, we soften, knowing that the people are devoted to us and will not listen to his conceited lies. Gbadu, the very first woman we created, approaches Awe to hear his false claims. With every lie he mutters, chaos ensues. The animals start to wonder if he can breathe Sekpoli, and the murmurings about Life begin. However, Gbadu sees through his dishonesties. She gathers the people, including her own daughter Minona, to go out and spread the word about us, to remain devoted and not to believe this monkey's deceitful claims.

We watch. We wait. For we know in peaceful serenity how this will end. Eventually, Awe believes his own falsehoods. He grows bold enough in his arrogance to climb the palm tree once again, and faces us. 'Mawu-Lisa,' he brazenly begins, 'I can breathe Life also. I want to show you and all of creation what power I have that matches yours.'

We smile. 'Go ahead,' we respond. We observe how he holds the clay figure of a bird in his paw, bores his eyes into ours with great defiance and blows. He blows and blows. The clay figure remains lifeless. We rise up. It is time to end this madness.

We move forward, floating above him, menacing. He shrinks back in horror. 'Do not worry, Awe, we just wish to offer this bowl of porridge. You must be hungry after everything that you have been up to.' He peers up at us, eyes darting between us and the bowl we are extending. He takes it tentatively, and drinks while shaking in fear. As he does so, we speak. 'Awe, you have committed a great wickedness against us. You have claimed to be more powerful than us. For this, you will be punished. For you have just consumed the seed of death, and the breath of Life will soon leave your body. It is only we who can create Life, but it is also only us who can take it away.'

We watch as the last breath leaves his body and he lays there still, lifeless. He is defeated and we, restored.

And so it goes. Breathe. Feel the air expand your lungs. Observe it leave your body. All the time remember that Sekpoli is the foundation of all Life. It can cleanse. It can renew. It can release. And one day it will leave you for ever and return to us. But hush now, for that is its beauty. It is your connection to us, to the place where your masculinity and femininity meet. It is the first and last thing you will do on this Earth.

Because what is Life, if not just one single breath?

Mawu-Lisa's World

The retelling above is based almost entirely on the oral tradition and teachings of the West African Vodun religion. This is one of the native belief systems of this region and it centres around the divine forces of nature, with a focus on the embodiment of spirit in all living things. The religion has adapted and developed from its more ancient origins and has spread throughout the world. When European colonists came to Africa, they brought with them Roman Catholicism, which combined with Vodun to create a new syncretic religion, one that remains popular today. An additional complication here is that Mawu-Lisa is also a major deity in the mythology of the Dahomey people, centred in the African nation of Benin. As such, Mawu-Lisa's roots are to be found in both the Vodun religion and Dahomey mythologies, in fact Dahomey is often cited as the culture from which Vodun originated. For a comprehensive view, we will explore both Vodun religion and Dahmonean culture in this chapter to situate our goddess fully.

Mawu-Lisa is a significant and intricate deity deeply rooted in the spiritual beliefs of the Dahomey people, a prominent West African civilisation that thrived in the region now known as Benin. We cannot know exactly how far back her worship dates to, but as the African roots of Vodun may stretch back over six thousand years, it is possible that Mawu-Lisa is one of the most ancient goddesses in our journey – contemporary even to our Inanna in the first chapter. She was worshipped as part of the Vodun religion in several regions of Africa – otherwise known as Voodoo religion. It is essential to understand that Vodun is diverse and can vary between different regions and communities, but certain core beliefs and practices are common throughout the Dahomey religious landscape. As Mawu-Lisa was worshipped across many different cultural contexts, I have chosen to focus on her as the main deity of the Dahomey people of Benin. It is this culture we shall explore in this chapter. If you have seen the movie *The Woman King*, you may feel some familiarity with it. *The Woman King* explores the Agojie military unit, a legendary all-female fighting force. I won't lie and say that watching that movie was not the first time I came across this culture. It sparked my interest and was one of the reasons I decided to delve into the worship of this amazing goddess and the people that revered her, and to investigate the historical truth. But before I go any further, I have to start with one of my caveats – or perhaps by now, rants – about the source material for this goddess and culture. Much of what we know about the Dahomey people has come through the eyes of white, Western, colonialists of the 16–1900s, and you don't need a degree in History to see how utterly problematic that is. These sources hail from several different nations, often European, and come with all the usual warnings about their interpretations and stereotypes about non-white societies and cultures. This is not to say that it isn't interesting or useful to examine such sources, because we will, but we must acknowledge up front the prejudicial lens through which the Dahomey people were observed.

The origins of Dahomey are complex, with legends and myths intertwining to form the tapestry of its early history. According to local lore, the kingdom was founded around 1645 by a king named Houegbadja. He established his rule in the Abomey Plateau, an area endowed with fertile soil and abundant natural resources, providing an ideal foundation for a thriving civilisation. This region lies within the central, southern areas of the modern country of Benin. In fact, this kingdom still exists today in the form of a constituent monarchy. They do not hold any official political power, but they still exert some influence. The kings do, however, maintain an important and central role in Vodun religious festivals and ceremonies. In its formative years, Dahomey was a realm of warriors and hunters, its people skilled in the arts of warfare and survival. The kingdom was founded by the Fon people, who are the largest ethnic group in the region of Benin, particularly in the south. The Fon people, like other neighbouring ethnic groups in West Africa, retained an oral tradition through the late medieval era, without ancient historical records. As such, it is hard to find authentic voices from this time period, hence why we have to rely heavily on the observations of European visitors.

What might it have been like in the society of the Dahomey? In this place, the political and social structures were more than just systems; they were the very fabric of everyday life, intricately woven with the values, beliefs and customs of the people. The capital of the kingdom, Abomey, was a centralised power, with royal residencies, artworks and bustling trade making it a vibrant centre. However, it was underpinned by the work of the people living around the city, in rural areas and villages. To gain a full picture, we must look at both aspects of the Fon lifestyle.

At the heart of Dahomey's political landscape, in Abomey, stood the *Ahusu*, the revered king who symbolised not just authority but also the cultural soul of the kingdom. The king wasn't just a ruler; he was a living embodiment of the people's heritage, their connection to the divine and the protector of Dahomey's rich traditions. His decisions echoed through the kingdom, shaping policies and ensuring the well-being of his subjects. Surrounding the king was a council of chiefs and advisers, individuals respected for their wisdom and experience. Together, they formed a circle of guidance, aiding the king in matters of governance, diplomacy and law. These advisers weren't distant figures; they were community leaders, approachable and familiar faces who understood the pulse of the people.

In Dahomey, society was structured by a hierarchy of power and privilege. Noble families, known as the aristocracy, held significant influence. These weren't just wealthy landowners; they were patrons of the arts, custodians of knowledge and pillars of the community. Their support for cultural endeavours, including music, dance and crafts, enriched the kingdom's social tapestry, ensuring that Dahomey thrived not just politically but culturally too. It was a patriarchal structure, but as we will see, there were some very interesting ways in which women were able to gain social status. The role of *Kpojito*, for example, carries a rich historical and cultural significance. Traditionally, the Kpojito, often referred to as the 'Queen Mother', has held a multifaceted position that combines religious, advisery and administrative responsibilities. The influence of the Kpojito has transcended time, and even in contemporary society, their role remains pivotal within the kingdom. Historically, the Kpojito played a crucial role in the religious landscape of Dahomey. Holding religious appeals, she was considered a spiritual figure, often involved in rituals and ceremonies that connected the kingdom to its divine roots. This spiritual connection was not only symbolic but also had practical implications, as the Kpojito would serve as a counsel to the king in matters of governance and decision-making.

One notable aspect of the Kpojito's role was their involvement in capital cases. Acting as an intermediary between the people and the ruling authority, the queen mother would plead on behalf of individuals facing serious charges. This added a layer of compassion and empathy to the justice system, as the Kpojito vitally ensured fairness and justice within the kingdom. One of the prominent figures in the history of the Kpojito title was Queen Hwanjile, whose contributions likely extended beyond her religious and advisery roles. Her legacy echoes through time, showcasing the significance of queen mothers on the cultural and political landscape of Dahomey. In the present day, the Kpojito continues to hold a position of influence within the kingdom's great council. This council, composed of esteemed individuals, is responsible for making important decisions and shaping the destiny of Dahomey. The queen mother's advisery role persists, reflecting the enduring respect for tradition and the acknowledgement of the wisdom that comes with age and experience. Moreover, the Kpojito oversees a substantial portion of Dahomey's day-to-day administration. This administrative role underscores the practical responsibilities that accompany the ceremonial and spiritual aspects of the title. The queen mother is not merely a symbolic figure; she actively contributes to the governance and management of the kingdom, ensuring its smooth functioning. The Kpojito's position among the Fon people of Dahomey is a testament to the intricate interweaving of spirituality, governance and tradition within their cultural fabric.

Another role of the queen mother was to oversee the militaristic aspects of Dahomean society. Of course, by this I mean the Agojie – or the Dahomey Amazons, as they were called by European observers. This term is problematic in many ways, most notably the blatant imposition of Greek mythological terminology upon a distinctly local tradition. It was commonplace at the time for white observers to use Greek mythology to describe new cultures, yet its colonial and – let's be real – often racist viewpoint needs challenging here. For obvious reasons, we will use the original name of these warrior women, as spoken in their own tongue, as the Agojie (please note there are a number of different spellings, but I have chosen, for clarity, to select just one). These women were renowned for their exceptional military skills and fierce dedication to protecting the king and the kingdom. Often recruited from the ranks of young girls, the Agojie were trained rigorously in combat, military strategy and physical endurance. They were entrusted with critical roles in both the defence and administration of the kingdom. The Agojie were considered the king's most trusted soldiers, and their loyalty was unparalleled. This earned them significant privileges and power within the palace and the kingdom. While serving the king in their military capacity, they also maintained their own autonomous organisation, led by a high-ranking woman known as *Gbeto*. This dual role allowed them to exert influence on both the political and the social aspects of Dahomey society. Imagine a time and place where it was the norm for men to be warriors, fighting battles and defending their kingdom. The Agojie were not your usual soldiers. They were unique because they are an all-female military unit. Their story began with a practical need: there were high casualties among men during battles with neighbouring groups. To fill this gap, women were recruited and coached to be skilled fighters, undergoing intense training, physically and mentally. These were not just ordinary soldiers; they were the king's elite bodyguards. In a time when women's roles were limited, the Agojie challenged traditional gender norms by proving that women could be fierce and capable warriors. These women fought in many wars, often against local rival tribes. In the latter half of the nineteenth century, they fought against the French in the Franco-Dahomean wars. The European observers who chronicled this noted that the women 'handled admirably' in hand-to-hand combat. Of course, as with many conflicts between indigenous and colonial invaders, the upper hand of artillery and riffles made a European victory inevitable, eventually leading to the establishment of a French colony that ended in 1960.

What made the Agojie even more remarkable was their involvement in political matters. Despite being warriors, they had access to the inner workings of the palace and participated in decision-making processes. This was highly unusual for women in that era, giving them a unique influence over the kingdom's affairs. Their significance went even beyond their military skills, as the Agojie were deeply connected to spirituality. They believed that their service was divinely sanctioned, and they played essential roles in ceremonies and rituals, invoking blessings and guidance for the kingdom. This spiritual connection added a profound dimension to their identity. Mawu-Lisa, as the supreme deity, featured highly in their worship. These women were not just warriors; they were symbols of empowerment and strength for women in Dahomey and beyond. At a time when gender norms were rigid, the Agojie stood as a testament to the unique agency, power and capabilities of women. Their story reminds us of the strength that comes from breaking barriers and defying expectations, inspiring generations to come.

Yet, Dahomey was more than its warrior women, rulers and nobility; it was a realm where the ordinary folk thrived. Villages, each with its own unique character, were the building blocks of the kingdom. In these close-knit communities, people knew each other by name, and a spirit of camaraderie filled the air. Take yourself back in time, stepping into the heart of a Fon village, where life unfolds amid lush fields and bustling activity, where the rhythm of life is dictated by the cycle of agriculture. Corn, cassava and yams, nurtured with care and devotion, form the backbone of their sustenance. These humble crops are not just food; they represent the collective effort of both men and women, who tirelessly sow the seeds of their livelihood. Picture the fields, where men toil under the sun, clearing and hoeing the earth, preparing it for the precious seeds. The women, with their hands skilled from generations of practice, delicately plant these seeds, knowing that their careful nurturing will yield the harvest that sustains their families. In this village, collaboration is key. Adult males unite, supporting one another in essential tasks like clearing land for cultivation and constructing sturdy homes. It's a reflection of their unity, a bond that strengthens the fabric of their society. And in the heart of their community, there are skilled artisans, each practising their craft with dedication. Male ironworkers fashion tools for their agricultural pursuits, ensuring that their fields thrive. Weavers bring life to fabrics, and female pottery makers mould clay into vessels that serve their daily needs.

Within the flurry of their daily lives, there is also a touch of mystique. Professional hunters, experts of the wild surrounded by supernatural reverence, protect their village. Their skills are not just a means of survival but a sacred duty, intertwined with ancient beliefs that add depth to their existence. In this vibrant Fon village, every action resonates with the spirit of unity, resilience and reverence for the land that sustains them. It is a place where families create the beating heart of their community. In these households, polygynous – men who have multiple wives – families are the norm, where each woman and her children find a place to call home within a shared compound. Zoom out a bit, and you'll see a network of these families forming a lineage. These lineages, made up of families connected through generations of male ancestors, often share not just blood but stories, traditions and a deep sense of belonging. At the helm of these lineages stands the eldest male member, a respected figure guiding the family with wisdom earned through years of experience. In the broader scope of the community, patrilineal clans played a significant role. These extended families, dispersed across Dahomey, were like vast, interconnected webs, weaving the tapestry of society. As time has marched on, these traditional clan structures have become less prominent, making space for new ways of community living and interaction. Yet, amid these changes, one thing remains steadfast: the reverence for ancestors. This ancient practice is the cornerstone of Fon religion. The spirits of those who came before are not forgotten; instead, they are venerated, their wisdom and presence still felt in the daily lives of the Fon people. It's a connection to the past that plaits a sense of continuity through generations, reminding everyone of their roots and the strength drawn from their ancestors' enduring legacy.

Yet, like any society, Dahomey had its challenges. Internal conflicts, though rare, were resolved through a system of justice that emphasised fairness and restitution, aiming for harmony rather than retribution. It was a reminder that even in times of discord, the underlying principle was to mend the social fabric rather than tear it apart. However, there was a dark underbelly to the seemingly peaceful society. Dahomey grew up during a time when the Atlantic slave trade was booming. Europeans saw Dahomey as a major source of enslaved people. Despite its internal stability, it was a society always ready for war. They fought against nearby groups and sold captives as enslaved people to Europeans. In return, they procured goods like guns, fabrics and alcohol. Some captives in Dahomey became enslaved people, working on royal farms or being sacrificed in ceremonies. These sacrifices were a source of particular interest to European observers, likely due to their fascination with the topic. One such ceremony was the Annual Customs of Dahomey, which involved gift-giving, religious ceremonies, military parades and discussions about the kingdom's future. Human sacrifices of enslaved people would take place, with up to five hundred people being sacrificed. The involvement of Dahomey in the transatlantic slave trade was central to its eventual downfall. In the 1840s, Dahomey faced challenges. The British pressured Dahomey to stop the slave trade, and in 1894, Dahomey lost to France in the Second Franco-Dahomean War. After this defeat, Dahomey became a French colony called French Dahomey. It gained independence in 1960 as the Republic of Dahomey, changing its name to Benin in 1975. You can see how difficult it can be to cut through these colonial layers to access the authentic voices of Dahomey.

Let us now move our attention to the religious beliefs

of these people. As we have already seen, Vodun is a traditional and indigenous religion that originated in West Africa. It is a complex belief system that encompasses a rich tapestry of spiritual practices, rituals and deities. Despite its misrepresentation in popular culture, Vodun is a profound and sophisticated religion that has deep roots in the cultural heritage of various West African communities. The origins of Vodun can be traced back thousands of years to the ancestral lands of the Fon and Ewe people in what is now Togo, Benin and parts of Nigeria. With the transatlantic slave trade, Vodun found its way to the Americas, particularly Haiti and the southern United States, where it underwent syncretism with other belief systems, giving rise to variations like Haitian Vodou and Louisiana Voodoo. At the heart of Vodun is the belief in a Supreme Being, often referred to as Mawu or *Nana Buluku*, who is the creator of the universe. Vodun is primarily focused on the veneration of a vast pantheon of spirits, known as *lwa*. These spirits are believed to govern various aspects of life, such as nature, fertility and justice. Each spirit possesses unique characteristics and powers, and devotees seek their guidance through rituals and ceremonies. Ancestor veneration is another crucial aspect of Vodun. Ancestors are considered to be intermediaries between the living and the divine, and their spirits are believed to influence the course of earthly events. Offerings, prayers and ceremonies are conducted to honour and seek the blessings of the ancestors, fostering a strong connection between the living and the deceased.

Vodun practices involve elaborate rituals and ceremonies, often led by priests or priestesses known as *Houngan* (male) and *Mambo* (female). These serve various purposes, including healing, protection and seeking guidance from the spirits. Drumming, dancing and trance-induced states are integral components of Vodun rituals, creating a vibrant and immersive spiritual experience. Sacred spaces are adorned with objects, representing the spirits and their attributes. Offerings such as food and drink are placed on altars as a means of honouring and appeasing the spirits. Sacred groves are also utilised for ceremonies and rituals, providing a connection to nature and the spiritual realm. Vodun has often been misrepresented in popular culture, perpetuating stereotypes and misconceptions. The association of Vodun with dark magic and harmful practices has contributed to the stigmatisation of this ancient religion. In reality, Vodun emphasises harmony with nature, community and spiritual balance, promoting positive values within its cultural context. Vodun is a resilient and enduring religion that has withstood the tests of time and cultural diffusion. Rooted in the traditions of West Africa, it continues to thrive despite external influences. By delving into the complexities of Vodun, we gain a deeper appreciation for the diversity and depth of spiritual beliefs that contribute to the cultural mosaic of our global society.

You can see now how prominent Mawu-Lisa would have been in historic Dahomey as the most powerful deity in Vodun belief. At its beating heart, Dahomeans actively engaged in the worship of our goddess, infusing it into their daily customs and rituals. Ceremonies and offerings were conducted to honour and seek her guidance. Devotees expressed deep reverence, acknowledging Mawu-Lisa as benevolent and caring entities, bestowing blessings of fertility, prosperity and protection upon their followers. Throughout Dahomey's history, the influence of Mawu-Lisa and Vodun was pervasive, shaping the cultural fabric and social identity of the Dahomey people. The legacy of their reverence for Mawu-Lisa has been transmitted across generations, forging a resilient and cherished spiritual herit-age. In the Vodun religious context, some women achieved elevated status, becoming powerful priestesses and oracles. They were believed to possess divine communication abili-ties and played crucial roles in performing rituals, offering sacrifices and providing guidance to the community. These priestesses were revered for their spiritual wisdom and often consulted on matters of significance, such as war, politics and health. Mawu-Lisa was an important deity to the Agojie women, providing them with guidance and protection.

Let's delve a little deeper into Mawu-Lisa. You may have noticed my use of 'we' and 'our' pronouns pronouns in the retelling. In fact, Mawu-Lisa is a highly complex and adaptable deity. At times, she is worshipped as just Mawu, the creator goddess with a distinctly female connotation. At others, Mawu is attached to Lisa and they come as a pair – in Dahomey as an older female and younger male consort. Most of the time, however, she takes on a female appearance. Sometimes, she is intersex, an amalgamation of Mawu and Lisa into one being. In my opinion, the best way to understand Mawu-Lisa is to consider the goddesses akin to the concept of Yin and Yang in Chinese thinking. Mawu represents the moon, femininity and night, while Lisa symbolises the sun, masculinity and day. Together, they embody the duality of all things in the universe. This duality is reflective of the Dahomey people's understanding of the balance that underlies all existence. It illustrates the interconnectedness and harmony of opposing forces in nature, where day follows night and masculine energies complement feminine energies.

Mawu-Lisa is considered the creator of the world and of all living beings, and they are revered for establishing the natural order and the principles that govern existence. The dualistic nature of the divine couple represents the contrast between light and darkness, good and evil, and the moral choices individuals face in their lives. This serves as a moral compass, guiding the Dahomey people towards virtuous behaviour and encouraging them to uphold the principles of justice, honesty and compassion. The symbolism of Mawu-Lisa is woven into various aspects of Dahomey society, from their creation mythology to the moral and spiritual values. According to Dahomey mythology, Mawu-Lisa shaped the earth, the seas and the sky, bringing order to the chaos of existence – a creative power that represents the generative force of the cosmos and the life-giving aspects of nature.

Consequently, Mawu-Lisa is associated with fertility and abundance and is an essential figure in rituals and ceremonies seeking blessings for growth and prosperity. The symbolism of Mawu-Lisa carries a profound message of gender equality. The divine couple highlights the equal importance of both masculine and feminine principles in the functioning of the universe. In a society that was largely patriarchal, Mawu-Lisa's existence provided a counterbalance. Remember the Fon village and the important role of agriculture in Dahomey life? In this agrarian society, the regular cycles of day and night, the phases of the moon and the changing seasons were all seen as manifestations of Mawu-Lisa's harmonious order. This emphasised the importance of living in synchronisation with nature and adhering to a balanced and virtuous way of life.

Mawu-Lisa also serves as benevolent and caring deities, providing spiritual guidance and protection to their devotees. The Dahomey people believed that by honouring and seeking the favour of Mawu-Lisa, they could receive blessings, healing and protection from malevolent forces. As a divine entity, Mawu-Lisa is regarded as an intermediary between the mortal world and the spiritual realm, allowing practitioners to communicate with the ancestral spirits and other deities. Mawu-Lisa is also regarded as the ancestor of the Fon people, connecting the living to their historical roots and lineage. This ancestral link reinforces the communal bond among the Dahomey people, emphasising the importance of honouring and respecting their shared heritage. Mawu-Lisa imparts essential ethical and moral values to the Dahomey people.

Mawu-Lisa has so much to tell us. Intertwined, both masculine and feminine energies as one being, a message is encoded. This message is a recognition that we all carry qualities that originate from both genders, and that we need both to be whole. That in the beginning, the masculine and feminine needed to cooperate to create the world. Now, I am not asking you to take this literally, but there is a powerful idea within this. We must ally the forces within ourselves, the seemingly opposing energies, to be truly whole. Much of what we know today, especially in Western cultures, has been determined by the social constructs that have been built. Through many cultural iterations, the notion of what is 'male' and what is 'female' behaviour has been cemented. The forcing of women into 'traditional' roles as housekeeper, mother and carer, and men as doers, breadwinners and pillars of strength. How utterly damaging! We seem to have forgotten a time where the individual counts, rather than predetermined tropes about who or what we are. The balance within, between these masculine and feminine energies, is unique to us all; a fingerprint. Who we are inside is totally our own. It doesn't care what our external gender is, or what society is constantly demanding of us. It wants to be free to draw upon the gifts that we have inside us, be damned which side they come from! It demands that we drop these labels and start to see all these traits as simply human ones. How many times have you seen parts of yourself, perhaps as a woman, and deemed them to be 'too masculine' and not acceptable to society? How many times have you toned down your passion in a meeting for fear of it being seen as 'aggressive' or 'overly assertive' by male colleagues? How often have you supressed rage inside yourself because anger is not accepted as a feminine trait? Similarly, how many times have men felt unable to express emotion in fear of being called 'too sensitive' or 'weak'?

Mawu-Lisa shows us a different path: a path of acceptance. We can make a stand, allow ourselves to be whatever it is we need to be in any given moment. We can be encouraged to challenge this absurd status quo. Like our Agojie, we can surprise the world by doing something different. Encourage others in their expression. Take a lead from the LBGTIQA+ community who have created a space where all are welcome, and notions of gender are entirely fluid and subjective. There is a little bit of Mawu and a little bit of Lisa in us all ... Embrace yourself fully and you'll find them.

SEDNA

Inuit Goddess of the Sea and Marine Animals

Sedna

*Inuit Goddess of the Sea
and Marine Animals*

The Betrayal

I knew that it was time. They had been coming to our house for years. First, I would hear their voices outside our igloo. Hushed sounds weakened by the strength of the icy Arctic winds. A sheet of pure white, so hazy that you cannot quite see anything around you. The bitter winds whip up around us, howling and raging. These snowdrifts can be brutal, the whiting out, the closing in. I shudder at how the weather is a reflection of the mood.

What I would always make out is the sound of the men conspiring, making decisions about my life. It fills me with such a burning rage, only the snow and ice around me can cool it. And now it is happening again. I pick up father's hunting mirror and hold it in my hand. I stare at my deep brown eyes, lined with thick dark lashes. I flutter them and tilt my face to the side to admire their length. I reach my hand back and begin to loosen the plait constraining my hair and watch as the long black strands of silk begin to fall around my face, down to my waist. I touch. I smooth. I caress. Next, I observe the glow of my skin, the flickers of sparkle and shadow that dance with one another as the flames of the fire roar in the middle of the igloo. All in all – and simply put – I am beautiful. I know this. It is what brings the men to my father's door begging for my hand in marriage. My beauty is therefore both my blessing and my curse. My thoughts are interrupted, and I throw down the mirror and conceal it beneath the furs that lay beside me. Father enters, wearing that look again. In this moment, I know that my time is up.

'Sedna, will you just meet with him?' my father pleads with me. 'He is offering so much – much more than the others.' For him, this is pure torture and I am an embarrassment. As a skilled hunter, my father is very well respected in our community. However, my insistence on not marrying is a source of shame for him. I can see the desperation in his eyes. I sigh. Perhaps it is time for me to do my duty as a daughter. I nod and reply using as few words as I can – I don't want him to think I am too keen.

'OK. Let him in.' He enters, and my first impression is that he is very handsome. Unusually tall, strong, with a lean stature and a commanding gaze. Long dark hair plaited behind him, flowing gracefully over his light grey furs. His eyes, mostly deep brown but with golden flecks of light, make him sparkle. He looks at me and bows his head.

'Sedna, thank you for allowing me to make my proposition to you. I know you have rejected many men from the community, so I come with something that I hope will please you.' He studies my reaction intently, but I am very good at keeping my feelings under the surface. He will read nothing in my eyes. He continues, 'I know your father provides many beautiful furs from his hunting expeditions and that you always have plenty of food to eat as well, and this pleases you greatly. What if I promise to lavish you in many furs, an abundance of food and offer great security and comfort? This is my promise to you.'

Now, my interest is piqued. No man has offered as much as he. I look him up and down, turning over his offer in my mind. But it is when I glance at father that my heart melts, for he is full of such hope that I cannot possibly let him down. I sigh. I look down at my feet. And for my father, I say yes. How was I to know this decision would be the end of me?

Many days and weeks have passed, and I have no sense of how long I have been here. Every single day is the same. I languish on this awful island – the home of my new husband. This place is barren; it is really only a rock floating in an ocean. There is no vegetation, just dry land, or the same land covered in snow and ice when the cold sets in. The waves lash ferociously at the shoreline; the ocean seems to be angry here, forever in turmoil. Occasionally I sit on the shore and drag my feet back and forth in the dust, gazing into the sea. I only have a few friends here, and they are disappointment, anger and sadness. Nothing is as expected.

After we married, my husband brought me here, to this island, cut off from my community. No livestock, no diversity of plant life, just the sea lapping at the shores and the terrible sound of birds. The day we arrived, he revealed his true form to me. I recoiled in horror as he rose up in front of me. I stood transfixed as he reached out his long arms and they began to sprout black feathers. His face became sharp and pointy, his nose protruding into a long beak. In what seemed to be a blink of an eye, he had become a bird, a spirit – non-human. I rushed at him, hands pounding at his chest, screaming at his betrayal. He looked down upon me, and told me that I had my furs and he will hunt plenty of fish, so he has kept his end of the deal. Since that day, we have eaten nothing but fish. With every rising and setting sun my spirit wanes and my soul groans as I mourn for a life lost. I pray at the shoreline that the gods will deliver me from this imprisonment. I watch the whales far out from the coast, observe them in their beautiful dance, as they flip and flop in and out of the water. A tear falls as my heart aches, desperate for the freedom the whales have.

One day, fate arrives. In the form of my father. I see him in his *qayaq*, his kayak, some way off the shoreline. First, I think I am going mad, that my broken mind is playing tricks on me. Then as he paddles closer and closer, I can make out the details of his kayak, and see the expression on his face. Concern. Anger. Betrayal. He arrives, pulling his kayak up onto the sand of the beach, and runs to me. He holds me in his sweet embrace and whispers into my ear, 'Sedna, I am sorry. I have come to bring you home away from this birdman.' He goes on to explain how news of my confinement was brought back to the community by some fishermen who spotted us from their boat. And then we paddle in the kayak, those harsh waves pushing into us as we strike at them with furious determination to get away from this awful place. The salty sea lashes our faces, stinging our skin and our lips. For each stroke forward, the ocean's current pushes us back two. We begin to tire, but just as we do, we have broken through the surf and we are able to paddle more freely as the waters calm around us. I stroke Father's arm. I can feel his trembling begin to subside.

But the birdman is a very powerful spirit and his rage at my abandoning him will be great. I look back at the island as Father paddles furiously to return us to our home, and what I see makes my whole body stiff with terror. The birdman is at the shore, looking bigger than usual, puffed up in anger. He is staring directly at me. But that is not what scares me most; what scares me most is who he is talking to. Just by his feet, lying in the waves that lap onto the shore, is a spirit of the sea. Hard to make out, transparent even, but unmistakable. I point her out to Father, who paddles even harder, fear swimming in his eyes, muscles tensed. I watch as the spirit of the sea turns, head out of the water, and sees us. And in the briefest of moments, she is gone. Dread. For now I know we are in serious trouble.

Before my mind has time to consider my situation, two huge waves, taller that the tallest of trees, loom in the distance. They race towards us with such speed. 'Father, look!' He turns his head just as the first wave hits us and the kayak is thrust under the water by the force of the impact. We twist and roll countless times before surfacing, only to be hit by the second wave, and down we go again, clinging on for our lives. I recall the whales dancing in the sea and observe the cruel irony that is life. We emerge once more, coughing up salt water, shaken, and now I understand what a broken spirit really feels like. When we recover, I look over to Father, who seems to be lost in thought, and I notice that his knuckles are white as he holds on to the paddles. And then I am back under the water. Another wave? I swim up to the surface, back towards the light of the day and to the shadow of Father's kayak. I emerge, gasping for air, eyes fixed on Father's, pleading for safety. I swim to the side of the kayak, latch my fingers on to its rim, expecting Father to pull me up into the safety and warmth of his embrace. Nothing. I bob there for a moment and look up at him. His eyes are glazed over, like a wild animal. He does not look at me, just into the distance. 'Father. Father!' I try to shake him out of his daze, but nothing. 'Father, pull me in!' Then I see it, concealed under his furs: his best hunting knife. I cling even harder. 'Please, Father, no! NO!' He ignores my cries. Saving himself, he takes his knife and cuts off my fingers. The last thing I remember before the knife slices off my fingers, before the pain sears through my body, before I become the dark, is how beautiful the deep blue of the sky is, and how I am never going to see it again.

Down. Down and down, I go. My fingers float down next to me, while seals, walruses and whales swim away. Away from wretched me. The light fades as I sink, deeper and deeper, overpowered by the betrayal of my father. Why would he do this to me? Forsake me in such a heinous fashion? I come up with nothing, only confusion and despair. Overwhelmed by the emotions consuming me – pure black hatred, pulsating anger and deep wells of sadness – I surrender. I give in to the feelings and allow the sea to take me.

My silky black hair swirls around me. I am the abyss. We are one. Now I float at the bottom of the sea, discarded, unloved and deceived. Sand at my feet, only the animals of the ocean for company. I can see the bases of great icebergs, huge blue walls of ice towering up above me, imprisoning me. Sometimes the animals come to me, seals, whales and walruses, observing my pain and attempting to nourish my soul with their presence and song. I have become their guardian, their keeper, and we have become as one. I love them as they love me.

The best days are when I can forget my pain, swim and glide in the icy waters with the whales, dancing and singing along with these majestic creatures. Sometimes, I feel something, perhaps a little bit of lightness. Yet my mood is as volatile as the tides, rage and sadness ebbing and flowing. At other times, as the sun's rays penetrate the waves, my watery world comes alive. I see glistening ice, dolphins dancing in the light and life so vibrant it fills my heart with warmth. Sometimes I inflict my fury upon the people and deny them the marine animals they rely on to keep alive, so they appease me, pray to me, make idols. And sometimes my heart softens, and I yield to their desires. But other times, the rage rises and I refuse. I watch as the people go hungry and experience just a fraction of the pain that torments me. And so it goes, I flit between pain and release, light and dark, love and hatred. Go softly, go gently. Swim towards the light in hope of salvation. I am slowly learning that I am not solely my pain . . .

Sedna's World

The above retelling is based entirely on the oral traditions of the Inuit people. As these people inhabitant a huge area, they have developed a rich cultural tradition of telling a variety of versions of the myths of Sedna. As such, I have woven together elements from different strands, many that have their origins in Greenland and surrounding areas. Despite there being many varieties of Sedna's story, most of them include the legend of Sedna losing her fingers in the sea, and most tales attribute this to her father. As such, I chose to make this the main focus of my own story.

The Inuit are a fascinating group of Indigenous peoples who call the Arctic and subarctic regions their home. They live in places like Greenland, which is a self-governing part of Denmark, as well as Arctic Canada, northern and south-western Alaska in the United States, and even a part of Chukotka in Russia's Far East. All in all, there are more than 180,000 Inuit people spread across these regions, each with their own unique identity and way of referring to themselves. In Greenland, they're known as *Kalaallit* (if they're from West Greenland), *Inugguit* (if they're from the Thule district) or *Iit* (if they're from East Greenland). In Canada, they go by *Inuvialuit, Inuinnaat* or simply *Inuit*. In northern Alaska, you'll hear the term *Inupiat*, while in south-western Alaska, they use *Yupiit* and Cupiit. Over in Chukotka, Russia, and on St Lawrence Island in Alaska, you might come across other names like *Yupiget, Yupik* or *Sugpiat*. As such, there are many distinct identities within Inuit culture and alongside them, many different histories and stories. When looking at Inuit culture in this chapter, we will focus on the Inuit living in the regions of Canada and Alaska, for the sake of clarity. I also need to raise a point here straight away. Some people outside of these cultures call the Inuit by another name – Eskimo. This is a highly offensive term to the Inuit, one that was attributed to them by white Europeans. The term became synonymous with eating raw flesh, and as such became a stereotype of the Inuit and denigrated their culture. In fact, the term Eskimo was widely used once Europeans colonised Inuit territories from around the 1500s, but now the term Inuit has been restored. Inuit roughly translates as 'the human beings' in Inuit languages. It is hugely important that we educate ourselves and use the correct terminology.

As this culture is both ancient and contemporary, we will discuss the current cultural practices of the Inuit and highlight traditional practices too. The source material for Inuit culture encompasses a diverse range of artefacts, documents and oral traditions that collectively provide insight into their history, lifestyle, beliefs and artistic expressions. These materials serve as windows into the unique world of the Inuit people, spanning their past and present, and offering a glimpse into their adaptation to the Arctic environment and the challenges they've faced over time. Archaeological excavations have uncovered artefacts and settlements that reveal aspects of ancient Inuit lifestyles and technological advancements, helping to piece together the puzzle of their historical journey.

Some ten thousand years ago, they travelled to the Bering Sea area. Around 1000 CE, a group known as the Thule people, who are the ancestors of today's Inuit in North America and Greenland, appeared in western Alaska. They had separated from the Aleut group about four thousand years earlier and had connections to north-eastern Siberia. As they moved east across the Arctic, they interacted with another group called the Dorset culture, or Tuniit in Inuktitut. Even before the Thule people, there were the Paleo-Eskimos (note terminology). Around 3000 BCE, they crossed the frozen Bering Strait, likely during winter. Later, around 2300 BCE, they migrated to the northern Canadian

Arctic, possibly due to changing climate. From there, they followed herds of game animals, eventually reaching Greenland, and forming different tribes along the way. It's a story of ancient migrations and adaptation, shaping the diverse cultures we know today. One of the oldest known Inuit archaeological sites was found on Saglek Bay and dates to approximately 3,800 years ago. Another was found on Umnak Island in the Aleutians, for which an age of approximately three thousand years was recorded. You can imagine, however, the practical and logistical difficulties of excavating in the Artic regions. As such, archaeology and anthropology combine to give us a timeline of the early migration and development of Inuit culture.

From where else do we get our information? The cornerstone of Inuit culture lies in oral traditions, where stories, myths, legends and historical accounts have been passed down. Elders play a crucial role in transmitting these narratives, ensuring the continuity of cultural knowledge. These oral traditions not only reflect Inuit beliefs, values and histories but also serve as a form of entertainment, education and community bonding. The Inuit are also skilled craftspeople. Inuit art is a powerful source material that captures the essence of their culture. Intricate carvings, sculptures, drawings and textiles are adorned with representations of animals, spirits, daily life and cultural symbols. These artistic creations not only provide a tangible link to their heritage but also serve as visual narratives that communicate stories and values. Many of these artefacts, however, have been stolen and showcased in museums in Canada and the United States, where, out of their original cultural contexts, they may be misinterpreted. This is all part of a wider discussion about the role of museums and their holding of precious artefacts – whether they ought to be returned to the country or people of their origin. Don't get me started on that, but it's important to make this point here! Back to what we were looking at – source material. In addition to oral traditions and art, the tools and technology used by the Inuit tell a story of adaptation and resourcefulness. Items such as kayaks, *umiaks* (skin boats), harpoons and intricately crafted tools showcase their mastery of survival in a challenging environment. These artefacts offer insights into their hunting practices, transportation methods and resource management techniques. As contact with the outside world increased through exploration and colonisation, photographs and written records by explorers, missionaries and anthropologists provided external perspectives on Inuit culture. These historical documents capture snapshots of daily life, clothing, dwellings and interactions with newcomers, shedding light on the evolving dynamics of Inuit communities. These sources contribute to a nuanced understanding of the complex interplay between tradition and modernity.

So, what do we know about Inuit culture and lifestyle? Consider for a moment what it might be like to try to survive in such harsh conditions. The Inuit are a highly adaptable people, learning how to shelter, hunt and thrive in these conditions. But you can imagine that nature is particularly cruel to human beings in such circumstances, and so much of Inuit culture is centred around this very real need to survive. The Inuit have forged a unique and intricate society deeply intertwined with their challenging environment. Over thousands of years, they have adapted to the harsh conditions of the polar region, mastering survival techniques and developing a cultural fabric that revolves around cooperation, resourcefulness and a deep respect for nature. The Inuit society, characterised by its nomadic lifestyle, innovative technology, kinship-based social structure and rich oral traditions, exemplifies a successful adaptation to one of the most extreme environments on Earth. Given the unpredictability of resources and the seasonal fluctuations in wildlife and plant availability, the Inuit adopted a nomadic lifestyle that allowed them to move in search of sustenance. They followed the migratory patterns of animals such as seals, whales, caribou and fish, setting up temporary camps in areas where resources were abundant. Mobility was crucial for survival, and their intimate knowledge of the land enabled them to navigate the treacherous terrain effectively.

In more recent times, the Inuit have had to adapt once again. Inuit communities continue to grapple with the effects of climate change that disproportionately impact their environment and traditional livelihoods. Melting ice, shifting migration patterns and unpredictable weather patterns have necessitated adaptations in hunting and

fishing practices. Inuit leaders are advocating for environmental stewardship and the preservation of their culture
and language to navigate these challenges. Technological
advances and introduction to money – something the Inuit
had no traditional concept of – has led to an abandonment
of nomadic living in favour of city life. Inuit ingenuity is
evident in their resourceful use of the materials available
in their environment. They developed a wide array of tools
and technologies to aid in hunting, fishing and survival.
One of the most iconic innovations is the umiak, a large
open boat covered with sealskin, used for transportation
and hunting in open water. Additionally, the invention of
the kayak – a sleek, one-person hunting boat covered in
sealskin – allowed for stealthy hunting of marine animals.
Modern technologies, such as the snowmobile, have per-
vaded Inuit culture and led to a shift towards less traditional
methods of living.

The social structure of Inuit culture reflects these conditions. The foundation of Inuit society lies in a complex
system of kinship, which organises relationships, responsibilities and social roles. Extended families, known as kin
groups, formed the basis of community and cooperation.
These kin groups shared resources, skills and knowledge to
ensure the survival of all members. Elders played a crucial
role, passing down traditional knowledge, skills and oral
histories to younger generations. It is unsurprising then,
that although men held high status is society as hunters,
builders, fishermen and travellers, women were equally

needed to keep the family alive through raising the children, cooking and crafting. As men travelled in search of resources, women would take on the traditional male roles. Hunting and fishing, cooking and preserving catches, tending to the children and home, trading goods such as clothes and tools as well as art, taking part in community meetings and importantly keeping Inuit stories alive through oral traditions. In the twenty-first century, however, social structures have changed significantly.

Let's take a look at changes for the Inuit in Canada as an example. Between 1800 and 1950, the way of life for Canadian Inuit changed significantly. They transitioned from self-sufficiency and independence to relying heavily on goods from Western countries, like clothing, food, weapons and tools. This shift happened because traditional hunting and trapping methods didn't generate enough income for the Western lifestyle. Market fluctuations and environmental concerns also affected their ability to sustain themselves. After the Second World War, the northern regions became part of Cold War defence plans, leading to the establishment of military and radar stations. While this created jobs and infrastructure, it forced many communities into sudden urbanisation, disrupting their traditional ways of living. Health crises, like polio outbreaks and declining caribou populations, further strained their resources. In response, the Canadian government provided social benefits and moved some Inuit families to new areas, both to address their needs and to assert Canadian sovereignty. In the 1950s, they became concerned about military security, discovering natural resources and addressing Inuit-specific issues. This led to the establishment of government departments and social programmes, aiming to support the Inuit population while also reinforcing Canadian control over the territory. The Inuit faced significant challenges as their way of life changed. Many struggled to maintain their cultural identity and history, leading to issues like alcohol and drug abuse. The suicide rate among the Inuit became much higher, and continues to this day. In fact, it is roughly three times higher in indigenous communities than in the rest of the Canadian population. By 2007, in an Inuit population of roughly thirty thousand, 40 per cent of the deaths were contributed to suicide in young males. There are many reasons that such tragedy befalls this community, but poor social mobility, economic hardship and environmental factors are said to be leading causes. Even in the early twenty-first century, Inuit communities still faced higher infant mortality rates and shorter lifespans compared to the rest of the country. Despite these challenges, the Inuit population has grown considerably since the 1960s, reaching over 65,025 people in 2016, spread across seventy settlements. Today, many Inuit make a living through fishing, hunting, trapping and creating artwork. Some work wage jobs, but social welfare and government support are vital sources of income for many. Traditional hunting and fishing methods have been preserved in only a few areas, with most Inuit communities adapting to modern ways of living.

In both early and modern Inuit culture, the sea is very important indeed, shaping nearly every aspect of Inuit life, from their subsistence strategies to their spiritual beliefs, and fostering a symbiotic relationship between the people and the ocean. Little wonder, then, that Sedna is such an important goddess. The sea provides a bountiful source of sustenance for Inuit communities. Marine life such as seals, whales, fish and sea birds are primary food sources, offering vital nutrients and calories needed to withstand the cold climate. This deep connection to the sea's resources is essential for survival in an environment where agriculture is nearly impossible and terrestrial wildlife is often scarce. The sea's fluid nature facilitated the nomadic lifestyle that characterises Inuit culture. With the ability to travel across frozen expanses during winter and open waters in the summer, Inuit were not tied to a single location. This mobility was crucial for following animal migration patterns, accessing seasonal resources and seeking shelter from shifting weather conditions. Mobility also fostered interaction with neighbouring communities, enabling cultural exchange and alliances. In addition, Inuit spirituality is intricately connected to the sea. Animistic beliefs hold that the sea is inhabited by spirits that demand respect and reciprocity. Shamans often communicated with these spirits to ensure successful hunts, protection from dangers and the overall well-being of the community. These shaman, or *anatquq*, would act as mediators between spirit and humanity, guiding people in their daily lives. They were also healers, in all ways that matter, physical, emotional and spiritual. With the spread of Christianity through European influence, many Inuit have chosen a syncretic approach, where they mix Christian and traditional ideas to form the basis of their belief systems. Whichever specific religion was followed, the spiritual connection reinforced ethical values of conservation and responsible resource management, ensuring that the delicate balance between human needs and environmental preservation was maintained.

Religion played, and plays still, a highly important role in society. Inuit mythology is a captivating web of stories, beliefs and spiritual practices that illuminate the intricate relationship between humans, animals and the natural world in the Arctic region. Rooted in animism, the foundation of Inuit mythology lies in the belief that spirits inhabit all living and non-living things, connecting the tangible and the spiritual realms. Through oral tradition, these myths are passed down, weaving a rich tapestry that explains the origins of the world, the behaviour of animals and the significance of natural phenomena. The mythology is not just a collection of fantastical tales; it's a living philosophy that shapes how Inuit people perceive and interact with their environment. Spirits, known as *inua*, are integral to this worldview, influencing daily activities like hunting and navigation. Shamans, revered for their ability to communicate with these spirits, play a central role in the mythology. Stories of powerful beings like Sedna, the sea goddess, and Nanook, the master of bears, encapsulate moral lessons and survival strategies, emphasising the importance of respect for nature and community cooperation. Inuit mythology isn't purely confined to religious rituals; it's entwined with daily life, guiding decisions and fostering a sense of unity with the environment. In an ever-changing Arctic landscape, this mythology endures, serving as a compass to navigate the complexities of existence while celebrating the profound interconnectedness between humans, animals and the spirits that shape their shared destiny.

Sedna mythology holds a profound significance within this framework, offering insights into the Inuit relationship with the natural world, their values and their survival strategies in the harsh Arctic environment. Sedna's mythology encompasses ecological wisdom, spiritual beliefs and ethical guidelines that have shaped the Inuit way of life for generations. The tale of Sedna reinforces the idea that respectful treatment of animals and the environment results in sustainable resources. The Inuit relied heavily on marine animals for survival, and the legend of Sedna underscored the importance of carefully managing these resources to ensure their availability for future generations. This ecological awareness is a timeless lesson that aligns with modern sustainability efforts, emphasising the need to harmonise human activities with the natural world. In addition, the story of Sedna encourages respect and empathy towards nature's inhabitants. Sedna's transformation from a young woman to a guardian of marine creatures denotes the interconnectedness of all living beings. Inuit communities recognised that their survival was intertwined with the well-being of the animals. Treating these creatures with kindness and understanding was believed to foster a positive relationship with the environment, leading to successful hunts and bountiful catches. This reverence for nature extended beyond practical considerations, reflecting a deeply ingrained cultural value.

Sedna's mythology also reflects the Inuit's spiritual connection to the world around them. Inuit animism holds that spirits inhabit all living and non-living things. Sedna herself embodies this belief as a guardian spirit of the sea. Her interactions with shamans, who communicated with her to ensure the community's well-being, highlight the bridge between the human and spiritual realms. This connection reinforced the Inuit's belief that their actions had consequences beyond the material world and that maintaining synchronicity with the spiritual realm was integral to their success and survival. There is also a rational aspect to her mythology. The legend offers an explanation for natural phenomena that shaped the Arctic environment. The howling winds that sweep across the region were attributed to Sedna's frustration and anger. This personification of natural forces provided the Inuit with a way to make sense of their environment's unpredictability: the perpetual despair at the betrayal of her father. This added depth to their understanding of the world around them, enabling them to navigate challenges and adapt to changing conditions. By attributing these phenomena to a powerful figure like Sedna, the Inuit contextualised their experiences within a larger narrative. In addition, the betrayal of Sedna by her father, which is just one version of many, could hint at us showing compassion and kindness to ourselves following traumatic events. We are encouraged to empathise with this goddess and in so doing may be able to turn this care inwards to ourselves.

Sedna's story is not just a tale; it is a fundamental part of Inuit identity. As Inuit communities faced external pressures, including colonial influences, her mythology became a touchstone for preserving their unique worldview. The lessons embedded within Sedna's narrative continue to guide their interactions with the environment, shaping their practices and reinforcing their cultural resilience.

Above and beyond all of this, Sedna carries another message for us. In my eyes, Sedna is an example of someone who uses her pain as a conduit. For at the heart of her story lies a betrayal – the ultimate betrayal of a father of his daughter. A pain so deep it lies in perpetuity at the bottom of a turbulent ocean. She lives with her pain, but at the same time grows to find some solace in her new life. She finds a path through her pain and trauma. In such a way, she can provide a message of hope, something that we have seen a great deal of evidence of in the Inuit community. She helps us to find the beauty in our pain, to give it space and perhaps with that expansiveness, to find solace.

I myself have experienced trauma, and a great many people reading this might recognise this feeling too ... That if you are able to embrace your pain, it softens, just enough that you can breathe. While we cannot fully escape the experiences that shape us, like Sedna we can have the courage to keep looking for the light, to keep reminding ourselves that hope is always there. That things change. Like the changing seasons, moving from a brutal arctic winter to a lighter and warming summer, we can learn to grow around our pain. Over time, it becomes only a small part of us.

Sedna is also an icon for the eco-conscious. Despite her heartbreak, she cares deeply for the environment and asks us to consider our own stewardship of this planet. Much like the goddess Artemis, Sedna is a powerful reminder of our ongoing relationship with this planet that we call home. Above all, she calls on us to respect our environment and acknowledge that we are indeed at its mercy. In a world where we seem to be under the illusion that we are separate to nature or, worse, able to dominate it, it is an important reminder that we are part of nature, and subject to it. Sedna's rage becomes our own for those who despair at the lack of care of the planet and the lack of urgent action from governments and those in power. We can both channel her anger and pay heed to her story to reconsider our own personal relationship with our environment. Perhaps her story will stir up in you a need for action, to reflect on what changes you would like to make. To interrogate your own choices.

Despite appearances, Sedna's story is actually about power. The power in us to choose how to respond to our pain. Our power to protect the environment and make changes. So, take back your power from the depths of your darkness. Use it to galvanise yourself towards freedom. In doing so, you might just find an inner peace that you thought was long lost . . .

HINE-NUI-TE-PŌ

Māori Goddess of the Night and the Dead

Hine-Nui-Te-Pō

Māori Goddess of the
Night and the Dead

The Shame

I was always the Dawn. The ethereal, pink-gold glow and promise of a new start. With every rise, there was the opportunity for cleansing, to start anew, to leave yesterday behind and be reborn. The welcome warmth and light after the damnation of the darkness. Life. I was renewal. I was hope. They called me the Dawn Maid. But that was then, and this is now.

As with most stories, mine begins with love. A great love. I was born of the first woman of our people, Hineahuone, or the Earth-formed woman. As a woman, I was revered for my ability to provide the pathway from which people enter the world, as are all women in our culture. I did not know my father. It is said that my beauty surpasses all others, so much so that other women were compared to me. People would say, 'You are Hine-tītama, the sight of you brings tears to our eyes.' They wept. I was that beautiful. So, I grew up in the glow of affection. Basking in the glory that was my shining youth. Blossoming into such beauty, wildly anticipating the adventure of my life. One day, the time had come. I was told it was time to find my match, to marry. To become a real woman.

He arrived, in a blaze of light which took my breath away. As my eyes adjusted, I saw him for the very first time, love fizzing in my heart from that first moment. It was Tāne, the god of light, forests and birds. He was huge, with rippling muscles and a strong chest. He wore his *piupiu*, the flax skirt, around his waist. His eyes were deep brown, with flecks of green. As god of the forest it was almost as if the green of the trees were dancing in these flecks. He even stood tall and firm, like the mighty kauri trees of our land. A perfect package. How could I know what that package was hiding?

Many years passed. Tāne and I lived in utter bliss in this stunning land of Aotearoa, the land of the long white cloud. A place so beautiful it hardly seems real. Dark turquoise waters in the north, lush and verdant forests bursting with ferns, dotted with sweet hibiscus flowers. The land is interrupted by huge mountains. Some lay still with their snow-capped peaks, others erupt with violent anger and spread their fires far and wide. The earth sometimes feels like it is bubbling. In the south, huge glaciers glisten in the sun, and the mountains get even more dramatic, coming together to form vast ridges and deep valleys. Lakes, like mirrors, reflect the beauty of the place.

We lay together in union, in these stunning lands, our love mingling to create our beautiful children. I screamed as I brought them into this world, pain searing through me so violently that I thought it might split me apart. But after the pain came something so new, something so visceral that it made me forget the agony. I held each child, touched their tiny hands and feet, watched intently as they opened their eyes for the first time. I soothed and hushed their cries and lost myself in them – so that I could no longer find where I ended and they began. Time passed. So fast I could barely notice it. That seems to be the way of happy times ... When you are immersed in them, you do not step back and honour how wonderful things are. You do not know that you must savour every last drop, because change is coming. And it might not go your way.

One day, something grew inside me: a burning, itching. It started small, almost imperceptible. But after a time, it grew and grew and irritated me so much, that I had to scratch it. I could not hold off any longer. Should I have left it alone, that curiosity? The need to know. Perhaps, but I cannot undo what has been done. So I left. I ran away from my family, deep into the lush green forests of my beautiful land, the land of the long white cloud, our Aotearoa. I sat, isolated, alone, only the burning inside me for company.

It festered. I ruminated. I obsessed. I sought solace in the trees, in the unfurling of the ferns around me, praying for my truth to unfurl inside me. I reflected: on my life, my children, but above all, on my identity. For the gnawing pain inside me was a yearning for my truth, for my origins. I wanted so desperately to know where I came from, and above all, who my father was. I whispered on the breeze, asking for the answer. I waited. Waited for the truth to set me free so I could return to my children.

I awoke, the hope of a new day dawning, the time when I am at my most luminous. I rolled over onto my back, and placed my hands behind my head, cradling it. My wavy brown hair flowed around me, like a river meandering around a rock. My long black eyelashes glistened in the morning glow, my eyes, a deep green, the colour of ferns. I just lay there, drinking in the essence of life. The essence of stillness. I listened. I heard the birds respond with beautiful song, as the light animated them. I focused on the sounds, the different bird species chirping in, the orchestra of life. Some long and low, others short and high, and one – just one – whose whispering was barely audible above the din. 'Come to me, little one, tell me what you have to say,' I called out. The little bird flew down from the branch above me and landed next to my leg. I sat up, eager to hear its message. I leaned in, close to the creature so I could hear it clearly. It was only tweeting one word, repeatedly. At first, I struggled to make it out over the noise of nature awakening around me, but then, as clear as the day that was just beginning, I heard it. And when I did, I ran.

I ran and I ran. So far. Down and down. Away from the glare of the sun. Away from its ostentation, its relentless burning. Away from the light that shines on truths, away from joy, away from happiness. I ran as far away from all life as I could, straight into the arms of death. Sweet darkness. I collapsed into its cold embrace and allowed shame to swallow me whole. Shame swimming inside me, filling me up, in the space where happiness had dwelt. Its bitter taste taking up residence in my mouth. Its heavy quality of self-hatred finding a new home in place of my heart. As all light left me, I sobbed as I realised I had seen my last dawn. There was no going back, no path to reclaim what I had lost, no respite from the shame I felt inside. My quest for the truth had cost me my dignity. That day, the Dawn Maid died and Hine-nui-te-pō, the Great Woman of the Night, was born.

And so, I sit here, hidden in shadows, their emptiness an outward expression of my inner world. Tāne came to find me after I ran away. Horrified to find me here, appalled that I would abandon my children, unable to fathom the deep shame I felt the moment I absorbed the words of that wretched bird. When the bird answered the prayer I had uttered, when it delivered the blow. When it told me that Tāne, my beloved husband, father to my own children, was also father to me. It had simply twittered 'Father' and the deep realisation of what was wrong, of the burning I felt inside, erupted in utter revulsion. Tāne could not understand that the shame was so great that I have become it. We are as one. He told me he had to have children with me, his own daughter, to ensure that the human species could be continued through our bloodline. He begged me to return, to raise our children, but I told him I would wait here. Wait in the dark. I haven't seen him since. I wait here for my children to return to me, the last glimmer of love left inside of me.

Down here, deep in the underworld, I get to work. I protect the newly dead as they arrive. Motherly instinct is dormant in me, but not yet fully extinguished. I nurture, I shield. I make sure the god of the underworld, Whiro-te-tipua, doesn't devour too many souls. For if he did, he could burst into the world, and it would be the end of all life. It is the memory of life that keeps me going here, the tiny corner of my heart that still allows in a crack of light. I recall those happy times, dancing in the light of the sun, my children's laughter bouncing on the breeze, the feeling of joy pulsating in my veins. But then, pain returns. I cry. I could fill oceans with my tears.

As I accept my fate, I allow shame to obscure me like the moon does the sun. I hide. In the shadows. I exalt in the dark. I rejoice in the dark red glow of the sunset. I linger at the border of light and blackness, waiting for the night, waiting for death. Meet me at the sunset, hold my hand as I guide you into the eternal night. I was the Dawn. Now I am the Night.

Hine-Nui-Te-Pō's World

Glorious New Zealand. I must admit straight away that I am a tad biased when it comes to the land of the long white cloud. I lived and taught there, and it has a place in my heart. I was fortunate enough to teach Social Sciences while in Auckland, and in doing so, I was immersed in Māori culture. I also learned a great deal from my students and colleagues and from my travels around the country. It is a fascinating culture, with a rich mythical history. Plus let's be real, it's an absolutely breathtaking place.

There will be a lot of terminology in Māori in this chapter. I don't want to overload you or ask you to learn all of these terms, but as the language is in danger of fading away, I felt it very important to do my part and honour Māori culture by using the proper terms. Finally, here comes one of my caveats. Māori culture is vast and diverse and ever changing. My hope is to give you a broad overview through which to access our goddess.

The roots of Māori culture trace back to the early Polynesian voyagers who navigated the vast Pacific Ocean to settle in what is now known as New Zealand, or Aotearoa in the Māori language. Māori culture is closely connected to Polynesian culture, especially within the Polynesian Triangle, which includes Hawaii, Easter Island (Rapa Nui) and New Zealand (Aotearoa). These cultures share language roots, religion, social organisation, myths and material traditions. Anthropologists believe all Polynesians originated from South East Asia and migrated across the Pacific Ocean. Recent research suggests that early Māori settled in the North Island of New Zealand around 1250–75, with similar estimates dating their arrival to 1280. During the Archaic period (around 1280–1450), the Māori relied heavily on the moa bird (a now extinct large flightless bird unique to New Zealand) for sustenance and brought edible plants like *kūmara* (sweet potato) to adapt to New Zealand's colder climate. They explored the land for resources, including stone for tools and materials like obsidian and *pounamu* (greenstone or jade). These stones played essential roles in their daily lives, such as food preparation, fishing and crafting. Early Māori artefacts, like a turret shell chisel and a pearl fishing-lure, link them to Polynesia. The discovery of obsidian from Mayor Island on the Kermadec Islands suggests return journeys between New Zealand and Tonga. As the Māori adapted to New Zealand's environment, they utilised local resources like pounamu, native timber and birdlife for tools, food and ornaments, leading to the development of the Classic Māori culture around 1500. European colonisation began around 1800, marked by encounters with explorers, whalers and traders. The Māori learned about firearms during these interactions. European settlement, Christian missions and trade followed, bringing significant changes to Māori society. The Māori adapted to new economic opportunities, focusing on horticulture and pastoral agriculture. However, the introduction of firearms during the Musket Wars

(1807–37) led to increased casualties and there was also significant population decline due to exposure to European diseases. The Māori population continued to decrease in relation to European settlers throughout the 1800s. In 1835, the Māori declared their sovereign independence, followed by the signing of the Treaty of Waitangi in 1840, which marked New Zealand as a British colony. Despite this, the Māori had limited representation in the early New Zealand parliament, leading to systemic racism and the suppression of Māori customs and values. Land ownership became a major issue, with Māori collective ownership transforming into individual land ownership under European influence. This significantly impacted Māori culture. In the twentieth century, urbanisation, land legislation and shifts in economic circumstances led to cultural changes among the Māori. A new generation of radicals emerged in the 1970s, advocating for increased Māori influence, the preservation of the Māori language and political rights. The introduction of a new voting sytstem, in 1996 gave minority groups more influence in politics, and the Treaty of Waitangi Tribunal began addressing Māori grievances. This resulted in financial settlements and the resurgence of Māori tribal organisations, leading to increased cohesion and control over assets. The repercussions of the Treaty of Waitangi and earlier European interaction with the Māori is a live issue in New Zealand. There are a number of socio-economic and health factor disadvantages that the Māori still face today: with issues like high unemployment, conviction rates, risk of serious diseases, poorer mental health outcomes and disproportionate educational opportunities.

When looking at Māori society and beliefs, we must discern between the modern Māori and traditional living. The lifestyle of the predecessors to the modern Māori would have been connected deeply to the land. This is not to say that this does not continue today, but with many Māori now living in urban centres, life looks a little different. What has remained, however, are Māori cultural beliefs, regardless of where or how someone might live. The teachings of Māori concepts are passed down within communities and families. *Te ao Māori* is the term used to refer to the Māori worldview, which is reflected in it cultures and traditions. It is different to the word *Māoritanga*, which is used to describe aspects of Māori culture. Simply put, te ao Māori is all about living your life within the boundaries of cultural, social and spiritual tradition and perceiving the outside world through this lens.

Central to Māori society is the concept of *whakapapa*, which can be loosely translated as genealogy or lineage. Whakapapa traces not only one's biological ancestry but also one's connection to the land and the cosmos. It highlights the interconnectedness of all living things and reinforces the idea that people are just one thread in the grand tapestry of existence. This concept plays a crucial role in shaping Māori identity, as individuals understand themselves not in isolation but as part of a larger whole. Perhaps one of the most recognisable and captivating aspects of Māori culture is the *haka*. This ceremonial dance, often associated with the All Blacks, New Zealand's national rugby team, is a visceral and intense expression of identity, power and pride. The haka is a manifestation of the warrior spirit that is deeply ingrained in Māori history, a call to summon strength and unity, and a tribute to those who came before. With stomping feet, fierce gestures and rhythmic chants, the haka resonates with a raw energy that transcends language, speaking to the heart of the Māori experience. Community also lies at the heart of Māori society. The extended family unit, known as *whānau*, forms the foundation of social structure. Within the whānau, roles and responsibilities are distributed based on age, gender and skill, creating a web of mutual support. The concept of *manaakitanga*, or hospitality, is deeply ingrained, emphasising the importance of welcoming and caring for others. Whether it's through sharing a meal, offering a place to stay or imparting knowledge, the ethos of manaakitanga fosters a strong sense of unity and shared responsibility.

Language is a crucial vessel for transmitting Māori culture and knowledge. The Māori language, *Te Reo*, is not just a means of communication; it's a living repository of ancestral wisdom, humour and emotion. For much of New Zealand's history, Te Reo was in danger of fading away due to colonisation and cultural suppression. However, in recent decades, there has been a resurgence of interest in revitalising and preserving the language. Efforts to integrate Te Reo into everyday life, education and media have helped ensure that the language continues to thrive and flourish, serving as a conduit for the transfer of cultural knowledge to future generations. Another iconic feature of Māori culture is the art of carving. From intricately carved meeting houses (*wharenui*) to elaborately adorned canoes (*waka*), Māori carving is a visual language that tells stories of creation, migration and important ancestors. The patterns etched into wood and stone hold layers of meaning, often illustrating tribal histories, genealogies and connections to the land. These carvings serve as physical links to the past, bridges between generations and markers of identity for Māori communities. Spirituality is another cornerstone of Māori culture. The Māori worldview is deeply intertwined with the spiritual realm, where gods, ancestors and natural elements intermingle. Tapping into this spiritual realm, *tohunga* (spiritual leaders) play a vital role in mediating between the physical and metaphysical worlds, performing rituals, healing and offering guidance to their communities.

What are the specific roles of women in Māori culture? Women have played a crucial role in Māori society, contributing to the cultural, social and economic fabric of their communities throughout history. The status and responsibilities of Māori women have evolved over time, reflecting the intricate interplay between tradition, colonial influence and modernity. In traditional Māori society, women held significant positions of authority and influence within their kinship structures. The concept of whakapapa, the connection of all living things through genealogy, underscored the importance of both male and female lineage. Women were highly respected as the bearers of whakapapa, as they were the ones who perpetuated the ancestral lines through childbirth. Moreover, the concepts of *tapu* (sacredness) and *noa* (commonness) applied to both genders, further highlighting the parity in their roles. Within the extended family, women were responsible for various crucial tasks that sustained the community. They were skilled in the art of *raranga* (weaving), which not only provided clothing and storage vessels but also transmitted cultural knowledge and stories through intricate patterns and designs. Additionally, women were integral to the gathering and preparation of food, utilising their deep understanding of the environment and its resources.

Leadership positions were not limited to men in Māori society. Women held the title of *ariki*, which denoted chieftainship, and could exercise authority over their own land and people. Ariki were responsible for diplomatic relations, making strategic decisions and upholding the *mana* (prestige) of their lineage. These women were highly esteemed, and their mana extended to their descendants, ensuring the continuation of their family's legacy. The arrival of European settlers and the subsequent colonisation had a profound impact on Māori society, including the roles of women. The introduction of Western norms and values often marginalised traditional Māori structures, leading to shifts in gender dynamics. However, it's essential to note that Māori women did not passively accept these changes; rather, they adapted and navigated new circumstances while holding on to essential elements of their culture. During the colonial era, Māori women demonstrated resilience and leadership in various ways. Many were vocal advocates for their communities, championing for land rights, education and social welfare. Women like Meri Te Tai Mangakāhia challenged oppressive policies and fought for Māori women's suffrage in the late 1800s, addressing not only gender inequality but also the broader issues faced by their people. As New Zealand underwent social and political changes, the role of Māori women continued to evolve. Urbanisation and the shift away from rural communities created new challenges and opportunities. Māori women entered the workforce, engaging in professions beyond their traditional roles. This transformation brought its own set of struggles, as women balanced work, family and cultural preservation in an ever-changing world. Today, Māori women continue to be pillars of strength within their communities. They hold leadership roles in politics, academia, arts and various other fields, contributing to the ongoing revitalisation of Māori culture and identity. The reclamation of Te Reo Māori has been significantly supported by Māori women, who recognise the language's role in preserving cultural heritage. They are instrumental in passing down traditional knowledge, stories and practices to the younger generation. However, it's important to acknowledge that challenges persist. Māori women, like their counterparts globally, still face disparities in areas such as education, healthcare and economic opportunities. Efforts to address these disparities and empower Māori women are ongoing, with community initiatives, advocacy and policy changes working to ensure a more equitable society.

Let's have a look now at Māori spiritual beliefs. Māori mythology is a rich and intricate tapestry of stories, beliefs and traditions that have been woven through the fabric of New Zealand's indigenous culture for centuries. Rooted in the deep spiritual connection Māori people hold with the natural world and their ancestors, these myths are not just tales of gods and heroes, but rather a profound reflection of their worldview and understanding of life. Within Māori religion there are a number of specific concepts that come together to form the basis of a Māori spiritual way of life. While Māori religious beliefs and practices can vary among different *iwi* (tribes) and regions, there are several core teachings that are commonly found in Māori spirituality. We have already met some of these terms, but to briefly recap: whakapapa is central to Māori religious beliefs. It refers to the interconnectedness of all living things through genealogy and lineage. Māori people believe that they are linked to their ancestors and the natural world through this lineage, creating a sense of belonging and continuity. Tapu refers to the sacredness or restriction associated with certain people, places or objects. Conversely, noa is the state of commonness or normalcy. These concepts guide how Māori people interact with their environment, emphasising respect for tapu spaces and practice. Mana is the spiritual power and authority that individuals, communities and even objects possess. It is earned through deeds, lineage and connection to the spiritual realm. The concept of mana influences social hierarchies, leadership and inter-actions within Māori society.

Māori religion includes a pantheon of gods, goddesses and supernatural beings that play specific roles in their cosmology. These figures are tied to natural elements, ancestral spirits and forces that shape the world. Central to Māori mythology is the concept of creation. In this narrative, Ranginui and Papatūānuku were locked in a loving embrace, and their separation by their children led to the creation of light, space and life as we know it. This separation represents the birth of duality and the balance that underlies all things in the world. Tangaroa, the god of the sea, is another prominent figure in Māori mythology. He is often associated with the tides, marine life and the rhythms of the ocean. His importance to the Māori people, who relied heavily on the sea for sustenance, is reflected in the rituals and ceremonies dedicated to him. Tangaroa's realm represents both the abundance of resources and the unpredictable nature of the ocean, embodying the respect and reverence the Māori hold for the natural world. Tāne Mahuta, the god of forests and birds, is revered as the an-cestor of humans. According to Māori mythology, Tāne crafted the first woman, Hineahuone, from clay, giving birth to the human race. His relationship with the forests highlights the interconnectedness of all life, as the trees, birds and people are seen as part of the same whakapapa (genealogy). This reverence for the environment extends to the practice of *kaitiakitanga*, or guardianship, which emphasises the responsibility humans have to care for and protect the land and its inhabitants. Ancestor worship is another significant aspect of Māori spirituality. Ancestors are revered and believed to be ever-present, offering guidance, protection and connection to the spiritual realm. Wharenui (meeting houses) often feature carved ancestral figures as a way to honour and maintain this connection. Tapu is often observed through practices such as *rāhui*, where certain areas or resources are temporarily restricted to allow them to regenerate. These practices reflect a deep respect for the land and its resources, ensuring their sustainability for future generations. Ceremonial rituals, such as *powhiri* (welcoming ceremonies) and *tangi* (funeral rituals), are essential aspects of Māori religious practices. These rituals strengthen community bonds, honour ancestors and acknowledge significant life events. I remember distinctly my powhiri when I started work at my school in Auckland – it was a deeply moving and warming welcome. *Wairua* refers to the spiritual essence that resides within all living things. This concept emphasises the connection of humanity and the environment, reflecting the Māori understanding of the world as a holistic, integrated entity. *Mauri* represents the life force or vitality that permeates all things. Objects, places and individuals possess mauri, and it is believed that maintaining this life force is crucial for overall well-being. Māori religion emphasises the interconnectedness of humanity with the environment. Kaitiakitanga, or guardianship, is a responsibility to care for and protect the land, waterways and living creatures. This concept aligns with the idea of reciprocity and respect for the gifts of the natural world.

In addition to these primary deities, Māori mythology features a myriad of supernatural beings and creatures. The *taniwha*, for example, are powerful water spirits. While some taniwha are seen as protective guardians, others are considered more malevolent and capable of wreaking havoc. These beings serve as metaphors for the unseen forces that shape the world and underscore the Māori people's respect for the power of nature. This also explains the Māori's deep affinity for the land; its ownership is a highly emotive and deeply spiritual issue for them. Mythology also extends to the realms of heroes and cultural icons. Maui, a demi-god and trickster figure, is renowned for his exploits and adventures. One of the most famous tales depicts Maui's attempt to slow down the sun, leading to the creation of longer days. His escapades, while entertaining, also carry moral lessons and convey the Māori values of perseverance, ingenuity and the importance of family bonds.

Within this framework, Hine-nui-te-pō is a prominent figure in Māori mythology and plays a significant role in their belief system. She is often referred to as the 'Goddess of Night' or the 'Goddess of Death', and her symbolism and significance are deeply woven into Māori cosmology and an understanding of life, death and the afterlife. While Hine-nui-te-pō is often associated with death, she also carries elements of transformation and renewal. Her realm can be seen as a place of rest and rejuvenation before the spirits are ultimately reborn into new life. In addition, Hine-nui-te-pō is sometimes depicted as the embodiment of the night sky, this symbolism connects her with the cosmos, stars and celestial cycles. Just as night gives way to day, her realm represents the continuous cycle of life, death and rebirth that is mirrored in the cosmic patterns. She remains today a powerful figure for the Māori and women in particular.

Hine-nui-te-pō is intertwined with the concept of whaka-papa, the interconnectedness of all living things through genealogy. For Māori women, this connection to ancestry is particularly meaningful, as they often play a central role in maintaining and transmitting family histories, traditions and cultural knowledge. In this way, the shame that Tāne is her father is reclaimed, reworked as a pride of illustrious lineage. For Māori women, this can serve as a source of empowerment, reminding them of their strength and resilience in navigating life's challenges and transformations. The teachings of Hine-nui-te-pō underline the cyclical nature of life, death and rebirth. In a world that often emphasises linear progress, her symbolism offers a perspective that aligns with Māori values of balance and harmony, traits that are often seen as feminine. This perspective encourages Māori women to embrace change, find meaning in cycles and appreciate the interconnectedness of all aspects of life. Hine-nui-te-pō's link to the natural world and her role as a guide to the afterlife reinforce Māori women's respect for the environment and their role as *kaitiaki* (guardians). This responsibility involves caring for the land, waterways and resources for future generations, inspiring Māori women to take an active role in environmental stewardship and the preservation of cultural landscapes. For Māori women, seeking spiritual guidance, wisdom and protection from Hine-nui-te-pō can provide a sense of comfort and connection. In the context of cultural healing and reconciliation, Hine-nui-te-pō's teachings can help Māori women navigate the impacts of colonisation, loss of language and cultural suppression. Engaging with this goddess can provide a source of strength and resilience as they work towards reclaiming their cultural heritage.

For me, however, there is another lesson we can take from our goddess, outside of her specific Māori context. Her story asks us to consider the concept of shame in greater detail. How many women have hidden in the shadows harbouring a great shame? In this story, Hine-nui-te-pō is forced to carry the burden of a shame that was not hers to hold. It is a story of how women have been shamed by men, forced into darkness, and overpowered by it. I am not suggesting that she is a victim, far from it, but her hand was forced. Her guilt was so heavy that she shied away from the light, concealed herself, made herself dark. She punished herself, gave up everything she loved. In my eyes, this is a metaphor for how it can feel to carry a shame that was forced upon you. Shame is a dark and heavy energy, one that keeps you hidden away from the truth of yourself. It is a leading cause of suicide, with sufferers so burdened and debilitated from shame that they are unable to reach out for support. What if we could reframe shame, and interrogate it further to see what lies beneath? Is this shame you carry really yours, or does it belong to your parents, friends, colleagues or wider society? What has made you feel so ashamed? If we consider for a moment that many people who identify as homosexual, non-binary or trans hide in shame as a result of their truth, afraid to step out into the world for fear of rejection or abuse, who does the shame belong to in this situation? It lies firmly at the feet of those individuals that have judged these people, cast them as wrong, as unacceptable, and are therefore the instigators of this shame. Why do we use the label 'coming out of the closet' to describe the process of these individuals simply being themselves? Why have we shrouded this moment in shame and concealment? Because societies and cultures have created this shame. I urge us to trace the shame we feel back to its origins. Whose shame is it really? Then we you can set it down, no longer carrying the weight of the expectation of others.

The shame of Hine-nui-te-pō isn't really a shame at all; rather it is her carrying the weight of her father's decisions and punishing herself for it. To embrace her story is to release your own shame. To find new power and purpose. To set down any burden you are carrying. To restore balance. To step out of the dark and into the light. For me, she represents the potential of emotional freedom. Take her hand, and you might just set yourself free.

HUITACA

Muisca Goddess of Rebellion, Sexual Liberation and the Moon

Huitaca

Muisca Goddess of Rebellion,
Sexual liberation and the Moon

The White Owl

I bathe in the blue-white light of the moon. I feel it as its glow illuminates my skin, as its ethereal quality swims around me, immersing me in pure and utter magic. I gaze up and observe its wholeness, examine all of the light and dark spots, marvel at its perfections and imperfections. It is me and I am it. I begin to float upwards, drawn in by the intoxication, up and up until the moon looms large in front of me. I am suspended in the cool night air, transfixed by the moon's beauty. I soar and glide, dark breezes bellow around me. It is then that I hear it, the rhythm of the night. It is calling.

I dive down, fast, and land in a great plateau in the Andes Mountains. These mountains are my home, their curves undulating on the landscape mimicking the curves of my body. Deep ridges and peaks rising high into the sky, sheer ravines covered in snow plunging downwards towards the earth. Into dense deep green forests, with air so pure you can feel it cleansing your lungs and replenishing your spirit. *Araucaria*, or monkey puzzle trees, dot the landscape, their spikey leaves home to many species of bird.

Among all of this, at the bottom of an open plateau, is where the people congregate. The noise here is deafening, but not as you might expect. It is not the chaotic sounds of nature or wild animals I can hear. It is the beat of the drum, the singing and the stomping of human feet. I rush towards the sound, exhilarated by the feeling in the air. I break into a run, unable to control myself. Across the great plateau I race, feet pummelling the ground. Moonlight illuminates my skin. I stop. There is a small pool of water in a clearing and I decide to cool my warm skin. I slip my hands in and cup the water in my palms, splashing it over my face. I caress the water's surface with my fingertips and the commotion begins to fade. The water resumes its glassy, smooth appearance. I peer into it, sitting with my legs to the side. The moon lights up my face and I look at myself. The people call me beautiful. I study my reflection as I see myself, properly. I am wearing my gold necklace, a deep yellow gold that was offered to me by the people. It is a beautiful serpent, its scaly, winding body around my neck, culminating in a head with protruding tongue that lies just about my breasts. My septum ring is also gold – a semicircle that pierces my nose. My headdress is a mix of gold and bright feathers, fanning out like the sun's rays. Our people are famous for their craftsmanship and skill with gold. It brings out the glow of my deep brown skin, the glisten of a setting sun. I look into my own eyes and understand why they call me beautiful. Dark brown eyes, like the bark of a tree, and dark brown hair that falls down my back all the way to the top of my buttocks. I do not wear any robes. For I am Huitaca, goddess of the free.

I stand. I run again. Towards the beat. I enter a clearing and my heart leaps at the sight in front of me. Everywhere I look I see the people, feet stomping to the rhythm of the beat, eyes closed in ecstasy, swaying to the music that floats on the night breeze. Men and women move together in beautiful synchronicity, like a mirror image of one another, the music pulsating through them like an unstoppable wave. Others are sitting around fires, drinking *chicha*, the intoxicating drink of our people. It is made by the women of the community. The women chew on corn and spit the mash into a clay bowl to start the fermentation initiated by their saliva. They then bury the covered bowl underground to keep it cool. After two weeks, it produces a thick yellowish, alcoholic concoction. We love to drink it.

I head over to a heap of human bodies, lying on the floor basking in the heat of the fire. Some are asleep in a stupefied state, the chicha in their systems. I join the group, take a mouthful from the wooden cup, and enjoy the feeling as the drink burns and stings my mouth as I gulp it down.

This is my way, everything in excess. Everything in the pursuit of pleasure. No boundaries, no rules – nothing to bind me. And the people love me for it.

I leap up, the buzz of the chicha pulsating through my veins, pupils wide as I react to the pure elation that comes with the drinking of this elixir. Suddenly, I feel the urge to join in with the dancing, and so I do. The beat and the drink work in glorious unison as I dance, moving my body freely and wildly in whichever way feels good. *Pleasure*. It warms my skin as I respond like a flower turning its head to bask in the power of the midday sun. This is what I am made for, to bring pleasure and joy to the hearts of our people. For the more I indulge, let go and allow myself to feel the power of extreme gratification, the more the people join in as well. I lead them in their desires, their need and refusal not to conform. To shake off the hard day's work in the fields, cultivating the crops. To unburden the day of intense crafting of goods; to release themselves from a day of raising the children, cooking and tending to the needs of the community. I exist to soften the experience that is the human condition, to provide some space to run to when life is too hard, too much. For them, I am freedom. For them, I am a sweet embrace. For them, I am wild abandon.

Don't get me wrong. I understand the need for rules. Our society is based upon them. Humans seem to need them to make the best of themselves. Do this. Don't do that. Be this way. Don't be that way. Expectations. All day. Everyday. When they come here, to me, under the glow of the moonlight, they let all this go. They come to me to reject the harshness of these structures, to explore what happens when they cross that boundary, into the wild. Into the untamed. Into the world of possibility. What they don't know is that they have become enslaved to their rules – no longer do they serve them, the rules have become their masters. They obscure the human spirt, and worse still, they crush it. When they come here, the spirit replenishes, and they remember themselves. They recall their truth. That rules are heavy. And people are light. So, we dance long to the night. Inhibitions lowered. Problems laid down. Expectations relinquished. Just us, the moon, chicha and the dance. Mingling together in heady pleasure. We writhe together, freely enjoying each other's bodies, for we are a sexually liberated people. Men have many wives, and women are highly regarded and respected. Here, the sexes come together and honour each other. For in feeling, humans can break free of the imprisonment of their minds.

I don't know how many hours have passed, but we are starting to fall into the blissful exhaustion that is the aftermath of intense enjoyment. Just as we begin to slip into a dreamlike state, the beat of the drums still ringing in our ears, I hear it. The unmistakable rush of water. Moving fast, trees snapping. I jump up and fly high into the sky. I float, and perch atop a mountain high in the Andes with a view of the plateau below. With terror, I realise what is happening. The River Funza, which runs through our lands, fortifying life with its nourishing waters, is running wild and free. Banks burst. River uncontained. I raise my hands to hide my eyes, but my curiosity means I cannot resist peeking through my fingers. The flood is swift and brutal. It crashes into homes, through fields and into temples. Destroying everything in its path. People flee, screaming. I thought that this was the worst thing that could happen. But how wrong I was.

He came. Like the angry wind. He came to me fast. He came to me in boiling rage. Bochica. My opposite. He taught the people the rules, morals and ethics. This society is his teaching in full colour, his creation. And now I have destroyed it with my wild ways. He stares at me hard and booms, 'Huitaca, you have gone too far. You have destroyed everything I have created with your lack of control. Your lust for everything.' I look down. I do not wish to defy him, for his anger is greater than my resolve. 'I will fix this. And then you will be punished.' He flies down, away. I watch from my vantage point as he directs the rough currents, as he creates a waterfall to curb their fury. This is how he creates the Tequendama Falls. The people are saved, their adoration of him restored. My power is weakened. For now, I know this must be the beginning of the end for me – the boundaries redrawn, the people retreating back into the safety and predictability of their rules.

Bochica rises and hovers in front of me. 'I said you would be punished and you will. For now, you will spend eternity locked in your refuge that is the night.'

So it is, I become what I am. A white owl. See me only

at night. Watching. Awake. Wide eyed. Alert. For I have found a way to exist and flourish in my form. I am the eternal queen of the night whose eyes embody the mystery of darkness. I fly, white feathers glistening in the moonlight in place of my dark skin. Yet I am still free, free to roam in the darkness. When you see me, watching in all directions, waiting for the pleasure to return, remember I live on inside all of you. This is not the end. For we will dance again.

Huitaca's World

I am not going to lie and say that choosing this amazing goddess was an easy one. Why, you ask? Because the historian in me was rather daunted by the source material for this wonderful figure. So much of what we know of Huitica has been written and passed down through the lens of the colonising Spanish. Unlike other goddesses in this book, I could lean on a wealth of archaeological material when the written record was scant. Yet, for Huitaca, even the archaeological record is incomplete. This was compounded by the lack of Western scholars writing about this culture and goddess, which led me to dust off my Spanish and get into the great work done by South American academics (thank you!).

Historically, the most prominent chroniclers who mentioned Huitaca were Catholics, Juan de Castellanos and Pedro Simón, both of whom were present during the early colonial period in Colombia. Castellanos, a poet and priest, wrote about Huitaca in his historical work *Elegías de Varones Ilustres de Indias*, describing her as a goddess associated with pleasure, beauty and joy. Pedro Simón, a Dominican friar and historian, referenced Huitaca in his work *Noticias Historiales de las Conquistas de Tierra Firme en las Indias Occidentales*, elaborating on her role in Muisca mythology. While the primary evidence for Huitaca comes from the Spanish chroniclers and the archaeological record, it is essential to approach the topic with a critical and culturally sensitive lens. As with any historical account of indigenous mythologies, there may be cultural biases and misinterpretations present in the Spanish writings. The story of Huitaca should be examined within the broader context of Muisca mythology and beliefs to gain a more comprehensive understanding of her significance in their culture. As such, I sought to restore her wild, sexually free and rebellious nature through my retelling, in line with what we know of Muisca thinking thanks to archaeological records. Let's get into that, shall we?

The Muisca people of Colombia, were an ancient civilisation that thrived in the Andean region from around the sixth century CE until the arrival of the Spanish conquistadors in the sixteenth century. Their history is deeply rooted in the highlands surrounding present-day Bogotá, particularly in the fertile plateau known as the Altiplano Cundiboyacense. Muisca society was highly organised and characterised by a complex political structure, an advanced agricultural system and significant metallurgical achievements. The Spanish conquistadors, led by Gonzalo Jiménez de Quesada, arrived in the Muisca territories seeking wealth and expanding Spanish dominion. More specifically, they were searching for the legendary El Dorado, the lost city of gold. Don't worry, more on that later! The Muisca initially attempted to resist the Spanish intrusion, but their technological inferiority and lack of unity eventually led to their subjugation. The Spanish conquest resulted in the downfall of the Muisca civilisation, and many of their religious practices and cultural traditions were eradicated or replaced by European customs. Despite the conquest, some aspects of Muisca culture survived, as indigenous communities preserved their ancestral knowledge, language and traditions. Today, the descendants of the Muisca people, along with other indigenous groups in Colombia, continue to struggle to maintain their cultural heritage while facing ongoing challenges related to land rights, environmental conservation and social integration. So, you can see where I am going with this. Some of what we know of this mighty civilisation has been passed down to us through the eyes of the Spanish colonialists, and as such comes with the usual warnings about the bias of a European lens.

As I've said, in order to paint a more authentic picture of these people, we must rely on archaeological evidence, which provides valuable insights into their ancient civilisation and helps us understand their way of life, cultural practices and technological achievements. Archaeological excavations have uncovered numerous Muisca settlements throughout the highlands of the Altiplano Cundiboyacense. These settlements often featured terraced agriculture and irrigation systems, indicating the Muisca's ability to adapt and cultivate crops on challenging mountainous terrain. The terraces were an advanced agricultural technique that allowed them to increase food production in their region. These agricultural innovations were crucial in sustaining their population and supporting trade networks. Findings of exotic materials and goods at Muisca sites suggest they engaged in trade with neighbouring indigenous groups and coastal communities, exchanging goods such as gold, textiles, ceramics and agricultural products. The Muisca were renowned for their exceptional metalworking skills, particularly in gold and copper. Archaeological sites have yielded an impressive array of intricate gold artefacts, including jewellery, ceremonial objects and figurines. These precious items reflect the Muisca's advanced craftsmanship and their religious and ceremonial significance. Pottery and everyday artefacts have also been discovered at Muisca sites. Pottery vessels were essential for food storage, cooking and ceremonial purposes. The style and design of these pottery pieces provide valuable cultural and chronological information about the Muisca civilisation. The Muisca had sacred sites, often associated with natural features like lakes, mountains and caves. These were used for religious ceremonies and offerings to their gods. Additionally, rock art, including petroglyphs and pictographs, have been uncovered at various Muisca sites, revealing glimpses of religious beliefs and rituals. Muisca burial sites have offered valuable information about their burial customs and funerary practices. Grave goods discovered in these sites shed light on beliefs about the afterlife and their social stratification. While the archaeological evidence has contributed significantly to our understanding of the Muisca people, it is essential to approach these findings with sensitivity and respect for their cultural heritage. Archaeologists work diligently to preserve and interpret these sites, recognising the importance of engaging with descendant communities and respecting their perspectives on their ancestral history. By combining archaeological evidence with the knowledge shared by indigenous communities, we can gain a more comprehensive and nuanced understanding of the rich and diverse history of the Muisca people. The picture that emerges is of a highly advanced civilisation, in similar standing to the perhaps better-known Aztec, Mayan and Incan cultures that surrounded them. I actually studied Mesoamerican archaeology at university and did not come across this amazing culture until I began researching this book. It is why I wanted to share it with you all and put it into the spotlight.

The Muisca territory was a land of contrasts. It encompassed fertile valleys, where the Muisca cultivated maize, potatoes, beans and other crops on those terraced fields, showcasing their agricultural prowess. Surrounding these valleys were imposing mountains and deep lakes, which held spiritual significance. In fact, it was through observing the religious and spiritual connection to lakes, in which the leader would adorn himself in gold, that the Spanish believed the Muisca people were the famed El Dorado culture. The heart of the El Dorado legend lay in Lake Guatavita, a stunning natural lake nestled in the Andean mountains. The Muisca people believed it to be a sacred site, and the ritual they practised there became the basis for the myth. The ceremony, witnessed by the Spanish explorer Juan Rodríguez Freyle, involved the newly crowned king covering himself in gold dust and precious ornaments before paddling out onto the lake. Once in the centre, he made offerings of gold, emeralds and other precious items to the gods, symbolising his wealth and power. The myth of El Dorado spread like wildfire among the Spanish conquistadors, fuelled by greed and the desire for fame and fortune. Conquistadors such as Gonzalo Pizarro and Francisco Orellana led expeditions deep into the Amazon rainforest in search of this fabled city. The quest for El Dorado became a symbol of the relentless pursuit of wealth and glory during the Age of Exploration. Countless expeditions were launched, entire fortunes were spent, and numerous lives were lost in the pursuit of this elusive city. Yet it remained a mirage shimmering on the horizon, always just out of reach. Many expeditions ended in disaster, succumbing to the harsh wilderness, diseases or conflicts with indigenous populations. As centuries passed, the legend of El Dorado transcended its geographical origins. It became a metaphor, symbolising the unattainable, the pursuit of an ideal that forever eludes our grasp. Writers, artists and filmmakers have all drawn inspiration from this captivating tale, weaving it into stories that explore the human obsession with wealth and the consequences of relentless ambition.

In the modern era, archaeological discoveries shed light on the Muisca civilisation and their rituals at Lake Guatavita. With the precision of modern excavation techniques, archaeologists delved into the soil around the lake. Among the treasures they unearthed were gold and emerald ornaments, meticulously crafted pottery and intricate textiles – each piece a testament to the Muisca's artistic finesse and deep spiritual beliefs. These artefacts, painstakingly catalogued and studied, painted a vivid picture of the Muisca's connection with the divine. Central to the archaeological revelations was the elaborate El Dorado ritual that the conquistadors had observed. Offerings, both exquisite and symbolic, were submerged – gold, textiles and ceramics sent into the depths as gifts to the gods. These offerings weren't merely precious objects; they were conduits between the earthly and the spiritual realms, embodying the Muisca's belief in maintaining cosmic balance. What emerged from the depths of Lake Guatavita was far more than artefacts; it was a profound understanding of the Muisca people's way of life. Their rituals were not mere ceremonies but intricate expressions of devotion, where nature and spirituality harmonised. Lake Guatavita was not just a geographical entity; it was a sacred space, a portal to the divine, where the Muisca believed their offerings could bridge the gap between worlds. These discoveries ignited a renewed passion for preservation. Efforts intensified to safeguard the remnants of this ancient civilisation. Archaeologists fastidiously documented their findings, unravelling the symbolism etched into each artefact. In doing so, they not only preserved the Muisca's legacy but also opened a window into a world where the boundaries between myth and reality blurred. It also restored the legend of El Dorado to its people, something I am big fan of.

So, what was this culture actually like? Outside of the legends of El Dorado, how were ordinary folk living? Allow yourself to picture walking through a Muisca village, a bustling settlement where families resided in traditional round houses, crafted from wattle and daub and crowned with thatched roofs. In the chilly Andean nights, these homes provided not just shelter but a warm embrace. Society buzzed with activity and purpose. Every individual had a role to play, a vital part in the intricate dance of their community. Artisans, their hands deft and skilled, expertly shaped precious metals like gold and copper into forms that seemed to capture the very essence of their beliefs. Imagine standing beside these craftsmen, watching in awe as they breathed life into these materials, creating not just objects of beauty but vessels of profound significance. These weren't merely adornments; they were conduits to the divine, intricate pieces of art that held the stories of generations, the wisdom of their ancestors and the hopes of their people. Each piece spoke a language of its own, telling tales of gods and heroes, of the sun and the moon, and of the deep spiritual connection the Muisca felt with the world around them. Amid the artisans, farmers toiled with the earth, their hands digging into the fertile soil, terracing high up into the Andean mountains. The verdant fields stretch out before you, a patchwork of vibrant greens and earthy browns. These farmers were more than just cultivators; they were stewards of the land, working in harmony with nature to coax life from the soil. Their crops, lovingly tended, became not just sustenance but a testament to their agricultural expertise. Maize stood tall, a golden promise of nourishment. Potatoes, in various hues, nestled beneath the earth's surface, patiently awaiting the hands that would harvest them. Beans climbed towards the sky, their tendrils reaching out like a community intertwined in mutual support. And then there were the traders, their footsteps echoing the heartbeat of the community as they ventured far and wide, bridging the gaps between distant communities. These adventurous souls traversed rugged terrains and winding pathways, carrying with them the treasures of the Muisca civilisation. They journeyed not just for commerce but for cultural exchange, returning with stories, beliefs and artistry from far-off lands, enriching the tapestry of Muisca society with the colours and textures of diverse cultures. Language was another essential aspect of Muisca culture and it also known as *Chibcha*. Although

their civilisation left no written records aside from picto-
grams, Spanish chroniclers who arrived later documented
their language and customs. Imagine speaking a language
that carries the stories and wisdom of your ancestors, passed
down from generation to generation. While the Muisca
language is no longer spoken today, traces of their ancestral languages still resonate in the customs and dialects of
indigenous communities in the region. It's like having a
connection to your roots, even if the words have changed
over time. Despite the challenges of the past, the Muisca
legacy endures today. Their profound connection to nature,
their remarkable goldwork and their belief in powerful
deities continue to capture the imagination of modern
audiences. The Muisca people have left an indelible mark
on the cultural heritage of Colombia, reminding us of the
richness and diversity of our world's history. Exploring their
society and culture allows us to delve into a civilisation that
thrived in unison with its environment. It also serves as a
reminder of the importance of preserving and respecting
indigenous cultures and traditions in the present day.

Women were powerful and essential members of the
Muisca community, making their mark in various aspects
of life. Just like in many societies today, Muisca women
played multidimensional roles, showcasing their strength,
wisdom and resilience. One of the most vital roles that
Muisca women held was in agriculture. They were skilled
farmers, working alongside men to cultivate crops that were
the lifeblood of their society. A Muisca woman would tend

to her maize plants, skilfully nurturing the crops that would feed her family and community. She knew the secrets of the land, the best times to plant and harvest, and her knowledge was valued just as much as any man's. But the influence of Muisca women extended beyond the fields. They were respected for their wisdom and often served as advisers to the ruling elite. Imagine a wise Muisca woman sitting with the chief, sharing her insight and helping shape the decisions that would affect the entire community. Her voice mattered, and her opinions were valued – proof that Muisca women were not just bystanders but active participants in moulding their society's destiny. In Muisca families, women held pivotal roles as mothers, wives and caregivers. They were the foundation of the household, nurturing their children with love and care. A Muisca mother would teach her daughters the art of weaving and pottery, passing down generations of artistic and cultural knowledge. She would instil values of respect, integrity and strength in her children, ensuring that these qualities would be carried forward into the next generation. Beyond their domestic responsibilities, some Muisca women even held positions of power and authority. As in any society, there were exceptional women who defied traditional norms and rose to leadership roles. These female leaders were known for their intelligence, charisma and ability to bring people together. In Muisca religious practices, women also played prominent roles. They were priestesses, performing rituals and ceremonies to connect their community with the gods. These women were seen as conduits to the divine, channelling spiritual energies for the betterment of their people. The Muisca recognised the unique contributions of women and valued their perspectives. Women were involved in decision-making processes, especially those that affected their families and communities. Their voices were heard in council meetings and discussions, and their opinions carried weight in matters of governance. Yet, despite their important roles, it is essential to acknowledge that Muisca women, like women in many historical societies, may have faced challenges and limitations. The patriarchal nature of the society might have restricted some aspects of their freedom and opportunities. But even in the face of this, Muisca women persevered, leaving an indelible mark on the fabric of their society. And this is one of the reasons that our fiercely rebellious goddess was revered so highly, for she was a goddess of their own hearts.

At the core of the Muisca religion were their gods, who held immense power over different facets of life. The Muisca believed that these celestial beings influenced everything, from the growth of crops to the cycle of life. These gods were not just distant figures; they were deeply ingrained in the Muisca's daily lives. To communicate with the gods and maintain harmony in their world, the Muisca relied on a class of religious figures known as *iraca* or priests. These priests were like spiritual mediators between the people and the divine. They performed rituals and ceremonies to honour the gods, seeking blessings and guidance for their community. They were widely respected and had far-reaching roles in Muisca society, including in political matters. It's like having wise and compassionate guides who help you navigate the complexities of life and connect you with something greater than yourself. Muisca religion also involved ceremonies that marked significant events in their lives. For example, they had rituals to celebrate births, marriages and deaths. Just as we have special ceremonies for important milestones in our lives, the Muisca held these events with great reverence, seeking blessings from the gods and protection for their loved ones.

Nature played a profound role in Muisca religious beliefs. The Muisca saw themselves as an integral part of the natural world, connected to the land and its rhythms. It would be like feeling deeply connected to the earth beneath your feet, the rivers flowing through the landscape, and the stars shining in the night sky. For the Muisca, nature was not just a backdrop; it was a living and sacred presence. This close connection with nature also influenced their religious practices. For instance, they performed rituals to honour the rain, seeking its life-giving powers for their crops. The Sun god, Sue, was a highly respected god, and in fact one of the most beautiful temples of the Muisca. It was decorated inside with golden *tunjos*, small figures made of gold or gold alloy. They have been found in the graves of the Muisca people, from all classes, as well as in temple structures to adorn them, and were buried in the earth as offerings. Some of these offerings would be for natural elements, like the Sun, Moon and earth elements. There was a deep appreciation for the wonders of the natural world, an acknowledging that we are all interconnected, dependent on the delicate balance of our environment. In many ways, the Muisca religion is a reminder of the enduring human spirit – the spirit that finds wonder in the natural world, seeks answers to life's big questions and finds solace and strength in the realm of the divine. In fact, you will probably see that this message is carried through most of the belief systems we have explored in this book. Maybe it is time for us to listen up.

Of course, our goddess Huitaca is part of this religious landscape. She was a goddess associated with pleasure, beauty and joy. She was known for her wit, wisdom and free-spirited nature, often depicted as a rebel figure challenging the norms of her time. Her worship was also connected with the goddess Chia, who symbolised the moon. Chia was worshipped all over the Muisca territories, but especially in the Moon temple in Chia, a city named after her. As a creature of the night, the white owl, Huitaca may have become connected to moon worship over time. In such a way, the worship of Huitaca may have taken place within Chia's temples. We cannot be entirely sure how the Muisca worshipped Huitaca, as the evidence we have is scant, meaning that finding her authentic voice is very hard indeed. Much like the goddesses we have already explored, a lot of her story has been passed down to us by her oppressors.

In Muisca mythology, Huitaca was eventually punished by the male gods for her rebellion and was turned into an owl, a creature often associated with darkness and mystery. But you cannot keep a good girl down, so she finds a way to adapt. This transformation represents the silencing of women who dare to challenge the status quo. As a creature of the dark, she is always present in the shadows, watching, and has become synonymous with the spirit of the Muisca. Despite her punishment, Huitaca's spirit lives on, serving as a source of inspiration for women today. Today, there is a belief in these regions that the energy of her influence remains in the spirits of her descendants. As such, women especially, who live in the former territories of Huitaca, carry her essence in them. In fact, in 2011, a Colombian photographer travelled the country's remote towns and settlements to find the daughters of Huitaca and to trace the ancestral connections of her descendants.

What else can our goddess say to us? Just as she resisted the constraints imposed on her, we can continue to challenge stereotypes, break barriers and demand equality. Reclaim control over our own sexuality, throw off the shackles of patriarchal constraint. As a story centred on sexual liberation and the pursuit of pleasure, we cannot gloss over this aspect. In a direct sense, Huitaca encourages women to reject society's constraints around their own sexuality. With the constant expectation of modern society, in this 'do this and don't do that' culture that pervades life, she reminds us that it's OK to do it our own way. That we are individuals as part of a collective, and that we should be empowered to feel free to express ourselves however we wish. That includes sexually – whatever floats your boat! Like our goddess Freyja, Huitaca demands that we see sex as something natural and sacred, not something to be vilified and concealed. More than this, Huitaca's story shows that even in the face of adversity, women have the power to rise above and reclaim their identity and voice beyond sexuality. In many ways, Huitaca embodies the spirit of resilience that defines the journey of women throughout history. Women have persisted, pushing for progress and paving the way for future generations. Women today stand on the shoulders of those who came before them, drawing inspiration from powerful figures like Huitaca, who refused to be silenced, who refuse to conform, who rise up against their oppressors.

Huitaca is a goddess for any woman – or man, for that matter – that chooses to make a stand when they feel their freedom is in danger. How can her spirit be channelled into everyday life? It is there whenever you choose to speak up against anyone or anything that threatens human expression. It is reporting racial, homophobic or misogynistic abuse in the workplace or on social media; it is teaching your children that rules need to be respected but questioned; it is getting involved in charities or activist groups; and perhaps most importantly, it is listening to that voice inside when it whispers that something just isn't right and doing something about it. In this way, I think we can take the story of Huitaca even further. Rather than just watching in the night, why don't we embody her true essence and speak up for what feels right? After all, just one voice can change the world. The story of Huitaca also teaches us the importance of embracing our true selves and celebrating our uniqueness. Huitaca's free-spirited and joyful nature shows us that it's OK to be different, to challenge convention, and to live life on our terms. So, be yourself. Unapologetically. Be free. Be loud. Be sexual. Be fun. Be wild. Rebel. Dance. Celebrate. Speak up against oppression. In short, be more Huitaca!

ISIS

Egyptian Goddess of Healing, Magic and Wisdom

Isis

Egyptian Goddess of Healing,
Magic and Wisdom

The Knowing

It began with opposition. Us and him. As is the way of this world. All of us born of the same mother and father yet divided. Separate. Pitched against one another. Destined to clash, to tear things apart. He is the one who threatened to take it all down, looming in the shadows, poised to destroy everything. Set. God of storms, disorder and violence. The angriest of us all. Why he hates us so is hard to fathom, but the hate is strongest for my brother-husband Osiris, ruler of these fertile lands. What is the origin of this hatred? It is hard to say, some say Osiris kicked him once, others say it is because Osiris lay with Nephthys, our sister, goddess of the air and head of the house, and consort of Set. But I think that this is just who Set is.

Born with a violent, chaotic nature, desperate to impose his darkness on the world of the living. Osiris stands for orderly rule, law, religion and farming. He would use any excuse to obliterate my Osiris. Order versus Chaos, a battle as old as time itself.

Something is coming, I can feel it. I sit here on the banks of the River Nile, the warm breeze caressing my dark skin, sticky sweat dripping. The waters, a deep shiny blue, trickle before me, calm today, ripples forming in the gentle winds. The reeds are dancing, making a soothing rustling sound. Dark orange mounds of earth rise and fall along the shores of the river, lush trees caressing its banks, the refreshing scents of cypress and eucalyptus floating on the air. Sands whip up in the distance. Egypt. My home. The beating heart of all life. This river. Sacred. I brush my hands along the tops of the reeds, enjoying the sensation as they graze my fingertips. I close my eyes and breathe in deeply, feeling the powerful energy of this place. The Nile, where all life begins and all life ends. For without it, Egypt would be barren. I slip off my sheath dress, lay aside my crown, which is adorned with a solar disk, and slide into the cool waters, naked. The water refreshes my clammy skin as I swim, as I cleanse, as I relax the muscles that are braced in fear of what is to come.

Now I sit, at the banks of the Nile, with tears flowing with such abundance that the river is flooding. Everywhere. Across the fields, watering crops providing life. Each teardrop falls into the rapids, water full, me empty. For I have learned what happened as I bathed in the waters; I have been told of the heinous act my brother Set has committed. While I relaxed, floating freely in these healing waters, he was being murdered. Osiris, the other half of me, my heart. Gone. Worse still, Set's rage compelled him to tear Osiris's body into pieces and fling them all over this blessed land. He breaks. I break. A hollow emptiness opens inside me, a deep black hole where something glorious used to sit. A knowing that it will never be filled, never heal and I am forever changed. For what am I without him? No future. Only a sorrow-filled past for company. Only wretched reminders on a constant loop, whispering to me that he is gone. And alongside him, a piece of me. Dead. For all eternity. And then, deep shock. I begin to shake and shudder. Panic. Fear. I am alone. I let out a scream so loud the lands around me shake, the birds flee from their trees into the safety of the sky, the animals run to save themselves. The people hide in their dwellings. My tears intensify as I collapse, into myself, into the ground. Hoping it will swallow me whole.

I lay like this for many days, or even weeks. Crying. Screaming. The banks of the Nile bursting, overflowing, swelled by my endless tears. Numerous visitors have tried to console me. First it was Nephthys, she came and smoothed my hair as I lay in the position of an unborn child on the soaked ground. She whispered kind words, offered to help find Osiris's body parts. I heard her words, but they passed through me as if through a pane of glass. As if I am watching myself from afar. Then Anubis, god of funerary rites and embalming, came. He said his knowledge could soothe my pain. But I batted him away. 'Not now,' I said. 'Leave me be.' Slipping in and out of consciousness, sweet sleep relieved me of my pain, only for it to sear through me again as my eyes fluttered open. Relentless. Unforgiving. Eternal.

Until one day, my tears began to dry. My mind began to find moments of calm, moments of clarity. So small, in the same way that the sunlight is able to pour through tiny cracks of a stone wall. It came like that. But it was enough. Enough to peel myself off the floor, to muffle the screams inside me. Enough to see that there is some action to take. An urge to search for Osiris, to reunite his body. Find him again. Hold him. Say my goodbyes. So, slowly at first, I began to walk. I decided to simply start. To get up, move and deal with everything else later on. I walked. I looked. I yearned. I flew. As a falcon, wide wings beating the air, I soared. Sharp eyed. Nephthys joined me, and we flew together. My strength grew with her by my side and my search intensified, growing more urgent. Emboldened by the anger that was beginning to boil within. Little by little, we found him. Scattered all over this bountiful land. With each piece I gathered, I let out a wail. Both in intense pain but also in intense relief. It was a confusing feeling, to have deep sadness and deep joy all at once. Still, we searched. And soon we had thirteen pieces, with only one to find.

*

I am back at the bank of the Nile, where my sadness and grief eternally swim. And now a fish. It comes to me as I sit, still searching for the final piece of Osiris. The fish speaks. She says she has eaten the last piece of him, she says she is sorry. 'Please forgive me, oh holy one.' I nod. Then I think, I think hard. As goddess of medicine and healing, I can fix this. With my magic, with my great knowledge, with my potent talents, I can solve this. I take the remaining pieces to Anubis in his great temple and we begin to piece Osiris back together. Anubis embalming, me speaking the magical words over the corpse. I pour every emotion into this process, channelling my insurmountable grief, weeping great floods of tears, raging at him for leaving me and lamenting how we will never again be in the sweet embrace of love, or have our own children. And it is potent. This heady mix of anger, grief, sadness, fear. I plead. I order him to return to me, but nothing. He lays there still. Life abandoned.

I return to the haven of my knowledge. To my magic. To my ability to heal. And I have it. I transform once again into a falcon, and hover above his body. And I beat, I beat my wings as hard as I can to send the breath of life into him. Just so I can feel the warmth of his skin, the strong safe embrace of his arms, the sweet taste of his lips just one more time. I beat my wings furiously. It works! His eyes open, he reanimates. His green skin grows deeper in colour and his long pharaonic beard restores to its former glory. I cry. He holds me. I savour every last drop of my time with him. We touch, making sweet love for a final time. And as I stare into his eyes, deeply into them, I see the essence of him. The light inside him, his soul. All the parts of his soul. In that moment, I find a peace. For although his time is up on this earth, he will never again walk the banks of the Nile, feel the heat of the sun on his face, touch those he loves or smile again, he will be free. In Duat. In the underworld. And so he leaves. He slips away again, and I feel the black hole inside throb once more. My powerful knowledge was able to resurrect him, but even I am not a match for the certainty of death. Yet I feel something new, something visceral. It is some kind of peace. Some kind of calm. A knowing that all things must come to an end on this earth. But there is more for us. For our souls. It is not really an end, but a transition. A change. In many ways, a beginning. And a beginning it was. For now, I am with child, a child called Horus. He will grow to be a mighty ruler of Egypt and avenge his father. So it goes. The cycle of life. What we borrow we must return, to be used again in renewal. We will meet again, in Duat. We will be together once more.

Find me. Down by the banks of the Nile. In the marsh, in the swaying of the reeds. When the waters flood, see my tears. When you experience loss, when the black hole opens up inside you, hush now. Allow me to wipe away your tears. Look beyond the darkness. You will see it. There is also peace. No true end, only transformation. That knowledge can be your salvation. That healing is possible. For this, I know.

Isis's World

The story of Isis and Osiris is one of the most well-known myths from Ancient Egyptian culture. The original source material for the legend comes from Ancient Egyptian religious texts, particularly the Pyramid Texts, Coffin Texts and the Book of the Dead. These are a collection of spells, hymns and rituals intended to guide and protect the deceased in the afterlife. The myth of Osiris and Isis is prominently featured in these funerary texts, offering insights into the religious beliefs and practices of Ancient Egyptians. Additionally, later classical sources, such as the works of the Greek historian Plutarch, provide information about the Osiris–Isis myth, as they were influenced by Egyptian culture and mythology. I have used a combination of these sources to compile my retelling.

I have left a whopper of a civilisation for our final chapter: Ancient Egypt, one of the cultures that first inspired my obsession with the ancient world. Fuelled by '90s classics such as *The Mummy* and *Stargate*, young me marvelled at the majesty of Ancient Egypt and I wanted to investigate more. Don't worry, I grew up and studied the culture, so I haven't got all the information from these movies! Ancient Egypt is a fascinating culture; away from the glamour of the pharaoh and the pyramid, everyday life was just as magical. We know a great deal about Egypt, owing to extensive archaeological interest in addition to source material from the Egyptians themselves, and the Romans and the Greeks – there is a lot. This chapter could genuinely be a book on its own, so I will attempt to give you an outline to get started with it.

Let's begin with a little history lesson. Of course, the origins of Ancient Egyptian culture pre-date what we will look at, with the society and civilisation changing and adapting over time. So, choosing a marked 'start date' for this culture is a little impossible. However, Ancient Egyptian history can be divided into several distinct periods, each marked by remarkable achievements in various fields. From the early days of the Old Kingdom to the foreign invasions of the Late Period, Egyptian history is a tale of cultural brilliance, architectural marvels and intricate religious beliefs. The history of Ancient Egypt begins around 3100 BCE when the region was divided into Upper Egypt (south) and Lower Egypt (north). King Menes, also known as Narmer, is credited with uniting these regions establishing the first dynasty and initiating the Old Kingdom period. The Old Kingdom (2686–2181 BCE) witnessed the construction of iconic pyramids, including the Great Pyramid of Giza, a testament to the Egyptians' advanced architectural and engineering skills. Following a period of decentralisation and disunity known as the First Intermediate Period, the Middle Kingdom emerged. This era saw the consolidation of Egyptian power, stability and cultural achievements. The pharaohs of the Middle Kingdom focused on improving infrastructure, promoting trade and enhancing the welfare of their people. Art, literature and religion flourished during this time, reflecting a rich cultural renaissance. The New Kingdom, around 1550–1070 BCE, marked a significant era in Ancient Egypt's history. It began with the expulsion of the *hyksos*, foreign rulers who had occupied Egypt during the Second Intermediate Period. The New Kingdom pharaohs pursued military conquests, expanding Egypt's borders and establishing an empire that reached its zenith under the rule of pharaohs like Thutmose III and Ramses II. This period also witnessed the construction of magnificent temples, including Karnak and Luxor, and the famous Valley of the Kings, where many pharaohs were buried. The New Kingdom gradually declined from around 1070 BCE due to internal strife, foreign invasions and weak rulers.

The Third Intermediate Period was marked by political fragmentation, with Egypt divided into smaller states ruled by different dynasties. During this time, foreign powers such as the Assyrians, Persians, Greeks and Romans exerted influence over Egypt. In 332 BCE, Alexander the Great conquered Egypt, initiating the Ptolemaic period. The last pharaoh of Ancient Egypt, Cleopatra VII, famously aligned herself with the Roman general Julius Caesar and later Mark Antony, in an attempt to maintain Egyptian independence. Egypt became a province of the Roman Empire after the death of Cleopatra and Mark Antony in 30 BCE, and the Romans brought significant changes to Egypt's administration, economy and culture. The Ancient Egyptian religion gradually gave way to Christianity, which spread rapidly during the early centuries after Christ. In 395 BCE, the Roman Empire split, and Egypt became part of the Eastern Roman (Byzantine) Empire. Of course, the historical picture is far more detailed than all of this, but hopefully this summary gives you a sense of the long and complex changes in Egyptian history.

How do we know so much about the history, I hear you cry? Our understanding of Ancient Egypt is derived from a diverse array of source materials, each offering unique insights. Hieroglyphic inscriptions, found on temples, tombs and monuments, provide detailed accounts of religious beliefs, royal decrees and historical events. *Papyri*, ancient rolls and codices written on paper-like material made from the papyrus plant, reveal everyday life through texts ranging from administrative documents to literary works and medical texts. Archaeological discoveries have unearthed artefacts, tools, monuments, pottery and art, shedding light on Ancient Egyptian technology, craftsmanship and artistic achievements. Mummies and burial sites offer a glimpse into Ancient Egyptian beliefs about the afterlife, preservation techniques and social hierarchy. Ancient Egyptian culture is also preserved in literature, including myths, stories and poetry. Additionally, wall paintings and reliefs depict scenes from daily life, religious ceremonies and royal events.

Ancient Egyptian language, one of the oldest and most fascinating languages in the world, was a complex system of hieroglyphs, logograms and alphabetic elements.

Hieroglyphs, the iconic script of Ancient Egypt, are intricate symbols representing objects, sounds or concepts. They adorned temple walls, tombs and monuments, providing a visual feast of religious texts, historical accounts and myths. Over time, the script evolved, leading to various forms such as *Hieratic* (a cursive script used for everyday writing) and *Demotic* (a simplified script for administrative and literary purposes). The Ancient Egyptians used their writing system not just for practical communication but also for religious rituals and preserving their cultural heritage. Hieroglyphs were believed to possess magical properties, bridging the earthly realm and the divine. Priests and scribes were specially trained to understand and interpret this complex language, ensuring the continuity of knowledge and religious practices. Decoding Ancient Egyptian language was a Herculean task for modern scholars. The Rosetta Stone, discovered in 1799, became a key to unlocking this ancient script. This artefact contained the same text in three languages: Greek, Egyptian hieroglyphs and Demotic. Using the Rosetta Stone, scholars like Jean-François Champollion deciphered the hieroglyphs in the early nineteenth century, opening the door to a wealth of knowledge about Ancient Egypt.

In order to gain a full picture of Ancient Egyptian life, we will need to look at many facets of its society. Let us begin with those at the top. The political system of Ancient Egypt was a complex and well-organised structure; a very rigid culture that evolved very little over time. It was characterised by a strong central authority, divine kingship and a hierarchical bureaucracy. The civilisation's political system was deeply intertwined with its religious beliefs, social structure and economic activities, creating a unique and enduring system of governance. At the top of the political hierarchy was the pharaoh, the ruler of Ancient Egypt. The pharaoh was not only the political leader but was also considered a divine figure, the intermediary between the gods and the people. Pharaohs were believed to be gods on Earth, possessing divine powers and responsible for maintaining *ma'at*, the cosmic order and harmony. The pharaoh's authority was absolute and unquestionable, and their decrees were considered the will of the gods. Succession to the throne followed a hereditary pattern, with the pharaoh typically passing the title to the eldest son. The dynastic system ensured continuity of rule within royal families, and pharaohs often married within their own bloodline to maintain the purity of their divine lineage. We see this within the story of our goddess Isis. The Ancient Egyptian state was highly centralised, with the pharaoh at the helm. The country was divided into administrative regions called *nomes*, each governed by a *nomarch*, who was responsible for local administration and tax collection. This term has Greek origins – if you were thinking it doesn't look very Egyptian, you'd be right! It derives from the Greek for district. The nomarchs reported directly to the pharaoh, ensuring the central government's control over various aspects of governance. Egypt had a sophisticated bureaucracy comprising scribes, priests and officials who managed the state's affairs. Scribes held a particularly essential role, as they were responsible for recording events, managing accounts and maintaining official documents. The bureaucracy was divided into different departments, each overseeing specific areas such as agriculture, taxation, construction and justice.

Ancient Egyptian society was hierarchical, with individuals categorised into different social classes. The pharaoh and the royal family occupied the top tier, followed by the nobility, priests and government officials. The majority of the population were peasants and labourers who worked the fields and contributed to the agricultural surplus, vital for the economy. Slavery also existed in Ancient Egypt, although it was not as widespread as in some other civilisations. In Ancient Egyptian society, enslaved people occupied a distinct and often challenging position. Slavery was not racially based; individuals could become enslaved due to various reasons such as debt, crime or being captured in wars. Enslaved people were primarily employed in labour-intensive tasks: working in mines, quarries, construction projects or agricultural fields. While they were considered property, some enslaved people could earn their freedom through years of faithful service. Slavery was a prevalent institution, yet the conditions and treatment of enslaved people varied widely. Some were well treated and integrated into their owners' households, while others faced harsh living conditions and backbreaking labour.

Despite their servitude, enslaved people were essential to the economy and infrastructure, contributing significantly to the construction of grand monuments, agricultural activities and other vital aspects of the society's functioning. However, contrary to the popular notion that enslaved people built the pyramids, archaeologists have concluded that it was likely a paid workforce that constructed them.

Allow us to explore the lives of regular folk in this society. Waking up in Ancient Egypt, thousands of years ago, you would be roused by the sound of roosters crowing and the warm golden sun rising over the vast expanse of the Nile River. For the Ancient Egyptians, life was intimately connected to the rhythm of the Nile, a lifeline that brought fertility and prosperity to their lands. Let's take a stroll down the bustling streets of an Ancient Egyptian city and peek into the daily lives of its people. As the day begins, families gather around a simple breakfast of bread (made from emmer wheat and barley), dates and perhaps some vegetables. The morning routine involved washing in the Nile or using a mixture of natron (a naturally occurring salt) and water. Ancient Egyptians valued cleanliness, and personal grooming was an essential part of their daily lives. After breakfast, it's time to head to work. Egyptians were skilled craftsmen, farmers and traders. Some worked in the fields, tending to crops like wheat, barley and flax. Others toiled in workshops, crafting exquisite pottery, jewellery and textiles. The papyrus reeds that grew along the Nile were used to create a variety of goods, including boats and paper-like material for writing. Skilled artisans and scribes were highly respected in society, and their craftsmanship adorned the tombs and temples of Egypt. Paintings depicted agricultural activities, fishing scenes and religious rituals. The Ancient Egyptians also excelled in sculpture, creating lifelike statues of pharaohs, gods and everyday people. The use of vibrant colours, especially in funerary art, added to the beauty of their creations.

Ancient Egyptian homes were typically made of mud bricks and had several rooms, including a kitchen area, bedrooms and storage spaces. Family was at the heart of their society. Families spent time together in the evenings, sharing meals and stories. Children, seen as blessings, played games with toys like dolls and carved animals. Education was also crucial, and boys often followed in their fathers' footsteps, learning their trade, while girls were trained in domestic skills. Lunch, the main meal of the day, was a hearty affair. Fish, a staple protein source, was abundant thanks to the Nile. Rich and poor alike enjoyed bread, vegetables like onions and garlic, and fruits such as figs and dates. Honey, a sweet treat, was used in cooking and desserts. Beer, a common beverage, was brewed from barley and enjoyed by people of all social classes. For the more affluent, wine was a delicacy.

Ancient Egyptians were deeply religious, and their daily lives were intertwined with spiritual beliefs. Every home had a small shrine dedicated to household deities. Daily rituals included offerings of food, incense and prayers to seek the gods' favour and protection. Temples, magnificent structures adorned with hieroglyphs and intricate carvings, were places of worship and community gatherings. In the evenings, after a day of hard work, people found time for leisure and entertainment. Board games like Senet and Mehen were popular pastimes, where you moved pieces in a way that may remind you of chess – in fact, you can buy games of Senet and Mehen today and give it a go . . . Music and dance were integral to Ancient Egyptian culture, with instruments like harps, flutes and drums providing a melodic backdrop to festive gatherings. Storytelling was also relished, with tales of gods, heroes and moral lessons passed down through generations. The ancient Egyptians loved to celebrate! Festivals were held throughout the year, honouring various gods and goddesses. One of the most significant celebrations was the flooding of the Nile, which brought fertile soil and ensured a bountiful harvest. This flooding usually occurs in the summer, after tropical rains swell the river fall. The *Wepet Renpet*, or New Year, was a joyous occasion marked by feasts, music and dancing. During festivals, people adorned themselves in colourful garments and jewellery, adding to the vibrant atmosphere. Life in Ancient Egypt was a tapestry of daily routines, spiritual beliefs and communal celebrations. The Nile River, with its life-giving waters, shaped the very essence of their existence. The Egyptians found meaning and purpose in their work, family and connection to the divine.

In Ancient Egyptian society, women held essential

roles, contributing significantly to various aspects of daily
life, culture and the overall functioning of the civilisation.
While their status varied based on their social class, wealth
and region, women in Ancient Egypt enjoyed a level of
independence and influence that set them apart from
their counterparts in many other ancient societies. Within
the family unit, women played a central role as wives
and mothers. Marriage was a respected institution, and
women were regarded as the cornerstone of a stable home.
Their responsibilities included managing the household,
overseeing the upbringing of children and ensuring the
family's well-being. In many cases, women owned and
managed property, which provided economic stability to
their families. Ancient Egyptian women had legal rights
that allowed them to own and inherit property, conduct
business transactions and even serve as witnesses in legal
matters. They could engage in trade, owning businesses
and managing their finances. Women of all social classes
participated in economic activities, working as weavers,
bakers and brewers, contributing significantly to the
economy. In religious contexts, women held important
positions. Some served as priestesses, performing rituals in
temples and participating in religious ceremonies. For example, the highly respected role of priestess of Hathor was
exclusively reserved for noble women. Hathor is a complex
goddess who oversaw many facets of Egyptian life, such as
the sky, kingship, joy, sexuality, maternity and femininity,
as well as death. These priestesses worshipped the goddess

at her temple near the Nile Basin and may have had at times several hundred attendants working alongside them. In fact, a mummy discovered in Thebes that dates around 2134–1991 BCE, has been identified as Amunet, a priestess of Hathor, who has become famous due to her unique and fascinating tattooed body.

It is not just Hathor that women would have worshipped. The Ancient Egyptians worshipped several goddesses, reflecting the society's recognition of the divine feminine. Goddesses like Isis and Ma'at stood for life, fertility and balance, emphasising the reverence Ancient Egyptians had for women. In religious rituals, women served as priestesses, musicians and dancers in temples, contributing to the spiritual ambiance of ceremonies. In burial practices, women were prepared for the afterlife with the same care as men. Elaborate funerary rituals and tombs adorned with intricate artwork depicted their societal standing and beliefs about the afterlife. Although formal education was more accessible to boys, some girls from affluent families received education in reading, writing and arithmetic, and those from the elite classes were known to engage in intellectual discussions, compose poetry and write letters. Women in Ancient Egypt were also skilled artisans, excelling in weaving, creating intricate textiles and producing pottery. They were similarly involved in the production of cosmetics, utilising natural resources for beauty products. Their creative talents extended to jewellery-making, where they crafted exquisite pieces from precious metals and gemstones, showcasing their artistic prowess.

And of course, I cannot skip over Ancient Egypt's most famous women. Hatshepsut, one of the most successful pharaohs, ruled Egypt during the fifteenth century BCE. She initiated ambitious building projects, including the renowned mortuary temple at Deir el-Bahari. Cleopatra VII, the last Pharaoh of Egypt, was a brilliant diplomat and linguist, infamous for her relationships with Julius Caesar and Mark Antony. The West defined Cleopatra by these relationships, in the common practice of diminishing female power by casting her in their shadow. In reality, Cleopatra was a shrewd and intelligent figure, asserting her power through clever liaisons and no doubt manipulations, to secure the future of her kingdom. Far from the temptress she has been portrayed as, she was a woman who knew what power she had and how to use it. Her reign, although tumultuous, showcased her political acumen and determination to preserve Egypt's independence. There is so much more to these women than the few words here – beyond their legends lie exciting and intriguing tales of fierce, accomplished women in a male-dominated world. Wouldn't it be great to take a peek behind those masks?

We have been introduced to Ancient Egyptian religion, but let's look at it a little more deeply. Ancient Egyptian religion stands as one of the most complex and enduring belief systems in human history. Rooted in a rich tapestry of myths, rituals and ceremonies, it profoundly influenced the culture, society and even the politics of Ancient Egypt for over three thousand years. This intricate religious framework revolved around polytheism, with a vast pantheon of deities embodying various natural elements, forces and aspects of life. There were major gods and goddesses such as Ra, the sun god, and Osiris, the god of the afterlife and rebirth. Hathor was revered as the goddess of love and music, while Thoth was the god of wisdom and writing. Each city or region often had its patron deity, and local cults and temples were dedicated to these gods. The deities were not remote and distant but were believed to be involved in daily life, influencing natural phenomena and human events. Worship involved a myriad of rituals and ceremonies. Temples served as the focal points of religious activities, but most people did not enter them and worshipped instead outside. The priests, a highly respected class, conducted these rituals, maintaining the sacred images, performing ceremonies and ensuring the deities were appeased. Offerings played a central role; the Egyptians believed that the gods needed sustenance just like humans. Offerings included food, drink, incense and various objects symbolising prosperity and fertility. These were also left in temples and tombs, believed to nourish the spirits of the deceased and ensure their welfare in the afterlife. The Ancient Egyptians held profound beliefs about the afterlife. Life continued after death, and the soul, often depicted as a bird, left the body after death. For this reason, preserving the body through mummification was crucial. Elaborate funerary rituals accompanied death, including prayers, spells and rituals performed by priests to guide the deceased safely into the afterlife. Tombs and burial sites were constructed meticulously to provide a comfortable and eternal dwelling for the soul. The deceased's possessions and favourite items were buried with them to ensure a comfortable existence in the afterlife.

Ancient Egyptian religion was deeply intertwined with the cosmos. The movement of celestial bodies, especially the sun and stars, held great significance. In fact, inscriptions on mortuary temples were placed in such a way that as the sun rose each day, its light illuminated the words. Ra, the sun god, was particularly revered, symbolising life, warmth and illumination. The daily journey of the sun across the sky and its nightly journey through the underworld were seen as metaphors for the cycle of life and death. The alignment of temples and monuments with astronomical events, such as solstices and equinoxes, underscored the religious significance attached to cosmic order.

The worship of the goddess Isis in Ancient Egypt and beyond is one of the most enduring and widespread cults in the ancient world. Isis, the divine mother, goddess of magic, nature and fertility, played a central role in the religious beliefs of Ancient Egyptians. Yet her worship was not confined within the borders of Egypt; it transcended geographical boundaries and time periods, leaving an indelible mark on the spiritual landscape of the ancient Mediterranean world and beyond. In Ancient Egypt, the worship of Isis was deeply rooted in the mythology of Osiris, her husband,

and their son Horus. The legend of Osiris, his murder by his brother Set, and his subsequent resurrection through the magic of Isis, became a central theme in Egyptian religious thought. This story symbolised the cycle of life, death and rebirth, providing hope for the afterlife and emphasising the nurturing and protective aspects of Isis. In Ancient Egyptian religious beliefs, the goddess Isis played a significant role in the context of the Book of the Dead, a collection of spells, rituals and incantations intended to guide the deceased through the afterlife in the face of the challenges they would meet. Devotees believed that her intercession could provide protection and assistance to the deceased, ensuring a safe passage to the realm of the dead and aiding in the judgement process before Osiris, god of the afterlife. The inclusion of prayers and invocations to Isis in the Book of the Dead underline her importance as a compassionate and benevolent deity, offering hope to the departed souls as they navigated the complexities of the afterlife. As the sister and wife of Osiris, Isis embodied the ideal Egyptian woman: devoted, resourceful and fiercely protective of her family. Isis was often depicted as a woman with a throne-shaped crown or as a mother nursing her child, emphasising her role as a mother goddess and protector of children. Her nurturing qualities endeared her to the Ancient Egyptians, and she was frequently invoked for assistance in matters related to child-rearing. Women, in particular, turned to Isis for guidance during pregnancy and childbirth, seeking her blessings for a safe delivery and a healthy child. Beyond her domestic and maternal aspects, Isis was also revered as a powerful magician and healer. Her knowledge of magic and herbal remedies made her a sought-after deity for those in need of healing and protection. People believed that she could cure illnesses, provide protection against evil forces and ensure a successful harvest. Her worship extended to all social classes, and her devotees included priests, pharaohs and common people alike.

The worship of Isis was deeply ingrained in the spiritual fabric of Ancient Egyptian society. Temples dedicated to Isis were centres of elaborate rituals and ceremonies. The Temple of Philae, for example, located on an island in the Nile River near Aswan, stands as one of the most significant archaeological sites dedicated to our goddess. The temple is a truly wondrous site, dating back to the Ptolemaic and Roman periods, with intricate carvings and inscriptions depicting rituals and offerings made to Isis. These historical layers of occupation have left evidence of Greek and Roman influences. It is easy to see why thousands of people were lured to the site to honour our goddess. Additionally, artefacts found within the temple complex, such as statues of Isis and votive offerings, reveal the tangible expressions of devotion by her worshippers. Devotees sought her blessings for various aspects of life and their worship of Isis often involved processions, prayers and offerings of food, flowers and incense. They believed in her ability to intercede on their behalf, providing healing, protection and guidance.

Pilgrims flocked to her temples, seeking solace and hope, and her influence extended far beyond Egypt's border – there was even a temple to Isis in what is now Germany. Isis's worship was characterised by a deep personal connection, with individuals turning to her in times of joy and despair, making her one of the most beloved and enduring deities in Ancient Egyptian religious practices.

As Egypt came under Greek and Roman influence, the worship of Isis spread throughout the Mediterranean world. The allure of Isis's mystery cults, promising a meaningful afterlife and spiritual salvation, attracted a diverse array of followers. These mystery cults, typified by secret rituals, initiation ceremonies and a deep sense of community, provided an intimate religious experience that resonated with those seeking a profound connection with the divine. Her cult may have enabled an aspect of social levelling that was unusual in classical culture. Isis's worship was likely to be popular among women, enslaved people and the travellers of society. She was a universal goddess, worshipped from Afghanistan to Britain, who was familiar to enslaved people, many of whom came from these further reaches of empire. Her compassionate and inclusive nature welcomed all, regardless of their social status or background.

During the Hellenistic and Roman periods, the worship of Isis underwent syncretism with local deities and religious practices. In Greece, she was associated with Demeter and Persephone, emphasising her agricultural and fertility aspects. In Rome, she was sometimes equated with Venus, the goddess of love and beauty, highlighting her nurturing and compassionate qualities. This syncretic approach allowed the worship of Isis to merge seamlessly with various religious traditions, making her one of the most widely venerated deities in the ancient world. Her symbolism and imagery found their way into early Christian iconography, particularly in representations of the Virgin Mary and the infant Jesus. The Madonna and Child motif, depicting Mary nursing baby Jesus, bore a striking resemblance to ancient depictions of Isis and Horus, evidence of the enduring influence of the Egyptian goddess on the visual language of Christianity. With the rise of Christianity and the subsequent decline of pagan worship, the worship of Isis gradually faded into obscurity. However, her legacy endured through the echoes of her symbolism in later religious traditions. Her compassionate, maternal qualities found resonance in the veneration of saints and the concept of the divine feminine within Christianity. If we are looking for a goddess that transcended time and culture, Isis may very well be the most powerful example.

What can we take from Isis today? Honestly, it is probably easier to look at what we *can't* take! As you can see, she was a total powerhouse of a goddess. Just like their ancient ancestors, for modern women, the figure of Isis holds significant value. Isis's story of overcoming challenges, including reviving her slain husband Osiris and protecting her son Horus, represents resilience, determination and empowerment – there is so much inspiration to be drawn from her ability to navigate adversity and emerge stronger. Isis represents feminine wisdom and intuition. In a world where rationality often takes precedence, her archetype encourages women to embrace their instinctive abilities and emotional intelligence. Trusting one's inner voice can be a powerful source of guidance, and it is often relegated in the noise of modern society. In a diverse and multicultural world, Isis's transcendence serves as a reminder of the universal thread that connects all living beings.

For me, though, there is something else in all this . . . Isis is also a keeper of knowledge. She owns it, nurtures it, and most importantly shares it with others. It is her knowledge of healing that gives new life to Osiris; her knowledge that is invoked by those completing funerary rites; her secrets that are sought after in a Greco-Roman world. In this way, we come full circle. To the end of our journey, where I believe I have left the best point until last. Through Isis, and in fact through all these formidable goddesses, you have empowered yourself in their knowledge. This would make Isis proud! I myself have channelled her by writing this book and sharing the knowledge I have acquired. For what is the point of knowledge, if it isn't shared? It is through our own education, expanding our horizons, that we reclaim the most sacred parts of ourselves. So find her. Down at the banks of the River Nile . . . hear her voice whispering to you through the ages. Take back this knowledge for yourself, nurture it, share it. Just like she did.

Final Thoughts

I don't know about you, but after all that, I need a good old cry and maybe even a scream. If that is you right now, then you have experienced the many emotional months I had writing it all! It is rather overwhelming to sit here and read the stories of these goddesses, to take in a global view of femininity through their eyes.

In each story, we see so much more than a myth; we see our own lives being played out. Our own history as women. These goddesses may not be real, but our own human emotion is, woven into the fabric of every single one, like a golden thread transcending time and space, travelling through cultures, to us today. Be honest with yourself now, how many of these tales felt like they were your own? How many times did you see yourself in these legends? My greatest hope is that I have achieved what I set out to do: to show you in real and tangible ways that you *are* your history. That the cultures and societies that have raised you were carved out by these great goddesses. And like every changeable thing, their message was lost through the ages, through the thousands of iterations that make up human civilisations. Their myths were adapted, moulded, censored or – worse – crushed by the male hands that held them. The message edited to suit the moral tale of a particular time, until it becomes unrecognisable. In truth, we have forgotten. We have forgotten who we truly are and the utter breadth of what we are capable of. We have forgotten to embrace ourselves and others wholeheartedly. We have forgotten to love every aspect of ourselves.

It's time to reclaim us, to reclaim who we really are. These goddesses are the tip of an iceberg – I want you to see the past as your greatest classroom. That in looking back, you find your original self. One that was unencumbered and free to be whole. The breadcrumbs are there, as I hope I have demonstrated in this book. Go and find them. Make your own rules for who you are and who you want to be. Take on life fearlessly. Regardless of your personal background, find these goddesses in yourself. Call them in. Embrace them all. See how your history has been shaped by women from all parts of the planet we call home. Notice how your femininity is mingled together by these figures, passed down to you through the passage of time. Will you hear their call?

Indulge me in an exercise. Grab a mirror and really look at yourself. Deeply into your own eyes. Feel the discomfort in trying to see your real self, and ease through it. Then watch as each of these goddesses appears as chapters of your own story. See the intricate narrative that is *you*, made up of traits and emotions that are the human condition. Observe your joy, your pain, your power, your light and your dark. See your wildness as Artemis, your darkness as Rangda, your sexuality as Huitaca and your wisdom as Isis. Observe how creation is expressing itself through you as Mawu-Lisa. Watch the parts of you that harbour deep shame like Hine-nui-te-pō, or hold on to resentment and pain like Sedna. Then reach into your shadows and behold your inner Kali. Get all sexy with it like Freyja. Finally, step back and see it all, in its glorious Technicolor like Inanna. Love it all. Accept it all. Honour it in others. Notice its utter beauty. For what you are seeing is life. All of life dancing in those eyes. Notice that you are a rich tapestry, uniquely woven together by personal experience. See how *you* are a Goddess with a Thousand Faces.

Select Bibliography

General

Baring, A., & Cashford, J. (1993). *Myth of the Goddess: Evolution of an Image* (New ed.). Penguin.

Budin, S. L., & Turfa, J. M. (2016). *Women in Antiquity: Real Women across the Ancient World*. Routledge.

Coulter, C. R., & Turner, P. (2000). *Encyclopedia of Ancient Deities*. Routledge.

Crerar, B. (2022). *Feminine Power: The Divine to the Demonic: The Citi Exhibition*. The British Museum.

Gimbutas, M. (1974). *The Gods and Goddesses of Old Europe, 7000 to 3500 BC: Myths, Legends and Cult Images*. Thames & Hudson.

Gimbutas, M. (1989). *The Language of the Goddess*. Thames & Hudson.

James, S. L., & Dillon, S. (2012). *A Companion to Women in the Ancient World* (Vol. 150). John Wiley & Sons.

Kutash, E. (2021). *Goddesses in Myth and Cultural Memory*. Bloomsbury Publishing.

Leeming, D., & Fee, C. (2016). *The Goddess: Myths of the Great Mother* (Vol. 56217). Reaktion Books.

Magoulick, M. J. (2022). *The Goddess Myth in Contemporary Literature and Popular Culture: A Feminist Critique*. University Press of Mississippi.

McHardy, S. (2023). *The Nine Maidens: Priestesses of the Ancient World*. Luath Large Print.

Motz, L. (1997). *The Faces of the Goddess*. Oxford University Press.

Ruether, R. R. (2005). *Goddesses and the Divine Feminine: A Western Religious History*. University of California Press.

Freyja

Brink, S., & Collinson, L. (2018). *Theorizing Old Norse Myth* (Vol. 7). Brepols Publishers.

Friðriksdóttir, J. K. (2020). *Valkyrie: The Women of the Viking World*. Bloomsbury Publishing.

Jochens, J. (2014). *Women in Old Norse Society.* Cornell University Press.

O'Donoghue, H. (2014). *English Poetry and Old Norse Myth: A History.* Oxford University Press.

Oslund, K., & Cronon, W. (2011). *Iceland Imagined: Nature, Culture, and Storytelling in the North Atlantic.* University of Washington Press.

Price, N. S. (2019). *The Viking Way: Magic and Mind in Late Iron Age Scandinavia* (2nd ed.). Oxbow Books.

Sigurdsson, J. V., & Kveiland, T. (2022). *Scandinavia in the Age of Vikings.* Cornell University Press.

Wikström af Edholm, K. (Ed.). (2019). *Myth, Materiality, and Lived Religion: In Merovingian and Viking Scandinavia.* Stockholm University Press.

Artemis

Blundell, S., Williamson, M. (1998). *The Sacred and the Feminine in Ancient Greece.* Routledge.

Budin, S. L. (2015). *Artemis.* Routledge.

Burkert, Walter (1996). *Greek Religion: Archaic and Classical.* Blackwell.

Ionescu, C. (2022). *She Who Hunts: Artemis: The Goddess Who Changed the World*. Tellwell.

MacLachlan, B. (2012). *Women in Ancient Greece: A Sourcebook*. Continuum.

Rhodes, P. (2005). *A History of the Classical Greek World: 478–323 BC*. Blackwell.

Rangda

Belo, J. (1966). *Bali: Rangda and Barong*. University of Washington Press.

Chemers, M., & Santana, A. (2022). *Monsters in Performance: Essays on the Aesthetics of Disqualification*. Taylor & Francis.

Crerar, B. (2022). *Feminine Power: The Divine to the Demonic: The Citi Exhibition*. The British Museum.

Goodlander, J. (2016). *Women in the Shadows: Gender, Puppets, and the Power of Tradition in Bali* (Vol. 89). Ohio University Press.

Geertz, H. (1991). *State and Society in Bali – Historical, Textual and Anthropological Approaches*. Brill.

Geertz, H. (2016). *Storytelling in Bali* (Vol. 304). Brill.

Slouber, M. (2020). *A Garland of Forgotten Goddesses: Tales of the Feminine Divine from India and Beyond.* University of California Press.

Inanna

Budin, S. L. (2023). *Gender in the Ancient Near East.* Routledge.

Collins, P. (2021). *The Sumerians: Lost Civilizations.* Reaktion Books.

Enheduanna., & Meador, B. D. S. (2000). *Inanna, Lady of Largest Hear: Poems of the Sumerian High Priestess Enheduanna.* University of Texas Press.

Frayne, D. R., Stuckey, J. H., & Beaulieu, S. D. (2021). *A Handbook of Gods and Goddesses of the Ancient Near East: Three Thousand Deities of Anatolia, Syria, Israel, Sumer, Babylonia, Assyria, and Elam.* Penn State University Press.

Helle, S. (2021). *Gilgamesh: A New Translation of the Ancient Epic.* Yale University Press.

Kali

Dalmia, V. (2017). *Hindu Pasts: Women, Religion, Histories.* SUNY Press.

Frazier, J. (2017). *Hindu Worldviews: Theories of Self, Ritual and Reality*. Bloomsbury Publishing.

Judge, P. S. (2014). *Mapping Social Exclusion in India: Caste, Religion and Borderlands*. Cambridge University Press.

Mitter, S. (1985). *Hindu Festivals*. Wayland.

Padma, S. (2014). *Inventing and Reinventing the Goddess: Contemporary Iterations of Hindu Deities on the Move*. Lexington Books.

Sharma, A. (2004). *Goddesses and Women in the Indic Religious Tradition* (Vol. 24). Brill.

Mawu-Lisa

Edgerton, R. B. (2000). *Warrior Women: The Amazons of Dahomey and the Nature of War*. Westview Press.

Landry, T. R. (2018). *Vodún: Secrecy and the Search for Divine Power*. University of Pennsylvania Press.

Leeming, D. A., & Leeming, M. A. (1995). *A Dictionary of Creation Myths*. Oxford University Press.

Lynch, P. A. and Roberts, J. (2010). 'Mawu', in *African Mythology* (p. 81). Infobase Publishing.

Anon. (2000). 'Mawu-Lisa and the shape of the universe', in *A Dictionary of African Mythology*. Oxford University Press.

Merkyte, I., & Randsborg, K. (2009). 'Graves from Dahomey: Beliefs, ritual and society in Ancient Bénin'. *Journal of African Archaeology*, 7(1), pp. 55–77.

Monroe, J. C. (2014). *The Precolonial State in West Africa: Building Power in Dahomey*. Cambridge University Press.

Sedna

Friesen, T. M., & Mason, O. K. (2016). *The Oxford Handbook of the Prehistoric Arctic*. Oxford University Press.

Kennedy, M. P. J. (1997). 'The Sea Goddess Sedna: An enduring pan-Arctic legend from traditional orature to the new narratives of the late twentieth century' in *Echoing Silence* (pp. 211–24). University of Ottawa Press.

Hulan, R. (2002). *Northern Experience and the Myths of Canadian Culture*. McGill-Queen's University Press.

Oosten, J. G., & Laugrand, F. (2010). 'Inuit shamanism and Christianity: Transitions and Transformations in the Twentieth Century' in *Inuit Shamanism and*

Christianity (Vol. 58). McGill-Queen's University Press.

Sonne, B. (2017). *Worldviews of the Greenlanders: An Inuit Arctic Perspective.* University of Alaska Press.

Stern, P. R. (2013). *Historical Dictionary of the Inuit* (2nd ed.). Scarecrow Press.

Hine-nui-te-pō

Denoon, D., & Meleisea, M. (1997). *The Cambridge History of the Pacific Islanders.* Cambridge University Press.

Mein Smith, P. (2011). *A Concise History of New Zealand* (2nd ed.). Cambridge University Press.

Te Kanawa, K., & Foreman, M. (1997). *Land of the Long White Cloud: Māori Myths, Tales and Legends.* Pavilion.

White, J. (2011). *The Ancient History of the Māori, his Mythology and Traditions.* Cambridge University Press.

Wonu Veys, F. (2010). *Mana Māori. The Power of New Zealand's First Inhabitants.* Leiden University Press.

Huitaca

Bruhns, K. O. (1994). *Ancient South America*. Cambridge University Press.

Carbonell, N. (1993). 'La mujer en la mitologia indigena colombiana'. *Revista Chichamaya*, 10, pp. 24–28.

Francis, J. M. (2007). *Invading Colombia: Spanish Accounts of the Gonzalo Jiménez de Quesada Expedition of Conquest*. Pennsylvania State University Press.

Gómez Londoño, A. M. (2005). *Muiscas: Representaciones, cartografías y etnopolíticas de la memoria*. Pontificia Universidad Javeriana.

Moore, J. D. (2014). *A Prehistory of South America: Ancient Cultural Diversity on the Least Known Continent*. University Press of Colorado.

Ocampo López, J. (2007). *Grandes culturas indígenas de América*. Plaza & Janes Editores Colombia S.A.

Vila Llonch, E. (2013). *Beyond Eldorado: Power and Gold in Ancient Colombia*. British Museum Press.

Isis

David, R. (2000). *The Experience of Ancient Egypt.* Routledge.

Green, R. L., & Copley, H. (1970). *Tales of Ancient Egypt.* Penguin.

Hollis, S. T. (2020). *Five Egyptian Goddesses: Their Possible Beginnings, Actions, and Relationships in the Third Millennium* BCE. Bloomsbury Academic.

Hornung, E. (1999). *History of Ancient Egypt: An Introduction.* Cornell University Press.

Laneri, N., & Steadman, S. R. (Eds). (2023). *The Bloomsbury Handbook of Material Religion in the Ancient Near East and Egypt.* Bloomsbury Academic.

Mazurek, L. A. (2022). *Isis in a Global Empire: Greek Identity through Egyptian Religion in Roman Greece* (New ed.). Cambridge University Press.

Teeter, E. (2011). *Religion and Ritual in Ancient Egypt.* Cambridge University Press.

Trigger, B. G. (1983). *Ancient Egypt: A Social History.* Cambridge University Press.

Acknowledgements

They say home is where the heart is, so I will start there with my list of gratitude! To John, my long-suffering husband, who is just as much a part of this journey as I am. For all the times you ferried tea, held me as I sobbed, championed me through the toughest moments – and for reminding me that I could do it when I doubted myself. For Ted, my little boy, I hope you read this and are proud of what I have achieved. So much of this journey is my way of explaining myself and the women in our lives to you. Then to all the people that brought me up because there were so many! For my darling Mum, who I have dedicated my first book to. This work is my ode to you, and all the aspects of yourself that you were not able to face while you were alive. I chose Isis for you specifically, as I'd like to think that you walk together now. For my second mum, Heather. Without you I would not be the woman I am today; thank you for all the love and support you have always given me, especially since we lost Mum. For Joy, who has always embraced me as her own child. These powerful women that brought me up are the inspiration behind these goddesses, I love you all.

Thank you also to the brilliant team at Dialogue – all of you have been truly amazing. Christina Demosthenous, my brilliant editor. Thank you so much for loving these goddesses from the outset and for getting them out into the world. It's been wonderful to be able to share their stories with you – I know you feel them as deeply as I do. You've been encouraging, patient and kind – more than I could ever have dreamed of for my first stab at writing. You are a true goddess and an inspiration. Powerhouse is my word for you! To my agents, Kirsty Milner and Hannah Ferguson, for believing in me and my vison. Nothing gets done without the damn right hardcoreness of a good agent, so thank you! Thanks also to the utterly talented Reiko Lauper for creating the most magical cover. Your artistry is breath-taking. Also, to D Lopez for revealing the faces of our goddesses to all, your work is simply stunning.

Finally, thank you to every reader out there holding this book. I truly wrote this *for* you and *to* you. I hope it has spoken to you and allowed you to see yourself more clearly. You have made this kid from the block's dream come true.

Bringing a book from manuscript to what you are reading is a team effort.

Renegade Books would like to thank everyone who helped to publish *Goddess with a Thousand Faces* in the UK.

Editorial
Christina Demosthenous
Eleanor Gaffney

Contracts
Anniina Vuori
Amy Patrick

Sales
Caitriona Row
Dominic Smith
Frances Doyle
Hannah Methuen
Lucy Hine
Toluwalope Ayo-Ajala

Design
Charlotte Stroomer

Production
Narges Nojoumi

Publicity
Henrietta Richardson

Marketing
Emily Moran

Operations
Kellie Barnfield
Millie Gibson
Sameera Patel
Sanjeev Braich

Finance
Andrew Smith
Ellie Barry

Audio
Alana Gaglio

Copy-Editor
Alison Tulett

Proofreader
Deborah Balogun